Praise for *The Radia*

Into a world desperate for healing and consumed by fear, *The Radiant Heart of the Cosmos* throws a wise and compassionate lifeline. By courageously sharing her own experiences, Penny Gill leads us into the depths of the heart center—"the royal road to awakening"—and shows us that by facing our suffering and fear, we open a portal to our wholeness and the only doorway to our future.

—Patricia Pearce, author of *Beyond Jesus: My Spiritual Odyssey*

Read it, reread it, and buckle up. *The Radiant Heart of the Cosmos* takes readers on a magnificent journey spiraling towards wholeness and away from the barriers imposed by the profoundly gendered categories and hierarchies we absorbed growing up. Penny Gill — a gifted writer, an irresistible teacher and a humane mystic — shows how openness to, and compassion for, one's own suffering develops the universal compassion that heals oneself, our fellow beings, and our world.

— Donal O'Shea, President Emeritus of New College of Florida, Professor of Mathematics and Dean of the Faculty at Mt. Holyoke College and author of *The Poincaré Conjecture: In Search of the Shape of the Universe.*

The Radiant Heart of the Cosmos is a profound, practical, personal and political treatise on transformation through meeting our fears and constrictions with kindness. Facing a world caught between disaster and rebirth, Gill's deep wisdom, expressed in an intimate human voice and in the voice of spirit guides, invites us to walk a path of healing for ourselves, each other and the planet.

— Rabbi Sheila Peltz Weinberg, co-founder of the Institute for Jewish Spirituality, author of *God Loves the Stranger* and the forthcoming *Let Us All Breathe Together*

Penny Gill has written a thrilling book, truly an adventure in consciousness, both deeply personal and immeasurably vast. Filled with inspired teachings, she weaves together three voices—her two Teachers, Manjushri and Kuan Yin, and her own voice. They invite us into the mysteries of the Spiral Path, a journey of healing and awakening that transforms fear and suffering, reclaims the Divine Feminine, and opens the heart for teachings about compassion and the cosmic Heart Center. Through her courageous inner work and guided by her Teachers, Penny gives us a soaring vision, filled with inspiration and hope. This wise and compassionate book is a gift for you and everyone you love.

— Olivia Ames Hoblitzelle, author of *Ten Thousand Joys and Ten Thousand Sorrows: A Couple's Journey Through Alzheimer's* and *Aging with Wisdom: Reflections, Stories, and Teachings.*

Devoted seeker and teacher Penny Gill invites the reader on her courageous journey from persistent lifelong despair to spiritual transformation. In emphasizing compassion as a way forward, she offers a path that can both soothe the savage internal beasts and, if applied widely, also help the healing of our ailing world in its current moment of peril and estrangement. "Either we break open our hearts to discover the fountain of compassion and kindness within," she writes, "or we literally destroy ourselves and our world."

— Paula Green, founder of the Karuna Center for Peacebuilding; Professor Emerita, School for International Training, Putney, Vermont

Manjushri, the Tibetan deity of wisdom, and Kwan Yin, East Asian deity of compassion, have offered the deepest wisdom to Penny Gill, this time on compassion, as the door to the heart center and from there, to higher consciousness. The path goes *through* suffering and crisis, and not away from them. And our ability to do so depends upon whether we can manage to welcome the profound feminine energy which living with compassion requires. The greatest spiritual teachers have brought us the same message—the Buddha, Confucius, Lao Tzu, Jesus of Nazareth, and our contemporaries such as Thich Nhat Hanh and the Dalai Lama, as Manjushri reminds us. They understand what life on earth requires. It is also the wisdom of the Apostle Paul: the ego must be crucified, so it can surrender to its greater Source. Only then can the inner Christ appear. Since humanity shapes the well-being of the Earth, this is decisive wisdom for creating a much healthier world, a world in which all might flourish. Penny Gill has given us a brilliant and persuasive gift here, which we all — and not least our political leaders — can use. The many crises we face also give us opportunities to wake up, and so, a dramatic shift in global consciousness.

— Helge Hognestad, Priest (retired), Church of Norway; Doctor of Theology, and author of many books, including *Gi sjelen rom, Bidrag til en fornyet Kristendom (2020) and Frigjore mennskets guddommelighet (2022).*

A profound and courageous book that speaks to anyone who yearns for personal and planetary healing. Read it quickly to expand your horizons or sip it slowly to open your heart and nourish your soul.

— Richard Sclove, author of *Escaping Maya's Palace: Decoding an Ancient Myth to Heal the Hidden Madness of Modern Civilization*

If you are a spiritual seeker longing to deepen your ability to recognize and respond to the Holy revealed within your own heart and the heart of the world, Penny Gill is a faithful and generous guide. With courage, wisdom, candor and deep kindness she takes us by the hand, leading us through fear into compassion and joy.

— Rev. Rachel Bauman, M. Div. Pastor and Spiritual Director, St. John's United Church of Christ, Madeline Island, WI

The Radiant Heart of the Cosmos

Compassion Teachings for Our Time

By Penny Gill

Housatonic
Massachusetts

Cover photo by Hendrik Zwart, Nordic Light Photo Tours
Back cover photo of Penny Gill by Seri Demorest

Cover and page design by Anna Myers Sabatini

Paperback ISBN: 978-1-7347571-4-9
Ebook ISBN: 978-1-7347571-6-3

Green Fire Press
PO Box 377 Housatonic MA 01236

Publisher's Cataloging-in-Publication data

Names: Gill, Penny, 1943–, author.

Title: The radiant heart of the cosmos : compassion teachings for our time / Penny Gill.

Description: Housatonic, MA: Green Fire Press, 2022.

Identifiers: Library of Congress Control Number: 2022900769

| ISBN: 978-1-7347571-4-9 (paperback) | 978-1-7347571-6-3 (ebook)

Subjects: LCSH Compassion. | Buddhism. | Conduct of life. | Spirituality. | BISAC BODY, MIND & SPIRIT / Inspiration & Personal Growth | PHILOSOPHY / Buddhist

Classification: LCC BF531 .G55 2022 | DDC 152.4—dc23

For my beloved Mount Holyoke College students,
women of wisdom and compassion

"If you bring forth what is within you, what you bring forth will save you.

If you do not bring forth what is within you, what you do not bring forth will destroy you."

—Jesus, from *The Gospel of Thomas*

Penny Gill, portrait by Marion G. Miller

Contents

The Radiant Heart of the Cosmos

Compassion Teachings for Our Time

An Invitation

You hold in your hands a collection of essays and Teachings from Manjushri, the great Tibetan Buddhist deity of wisdom and compassion, and Kwan Yin, the Buddhist deity of compassion. These Teachings, which have engaged me so powerfully, will give you a glimpse of the courteous, relentless, and always kindly instruction I have received, and how they have been embedded in our Teacher/student relationships of many years. The Teachings are often deeply personal, as each responds to something vivid and pressing in my own life. And you will recognize that virtually everything here is part of a conversation.

Over the many years of this work, the original strangeness and unpredictability dissolved, in favor of deep trust and openness and freedom. Day by day, month by month, despite all I could not understand, these encounters changed me profoundly. I long for you too to receive this astonishing gift of healing and insight; of compassion and wisdom.

Isn't that what a spiritual life is about? And for?

I think so. It is how we become fully human. And its central practice is relatedness. Conversation or dialogue—the kind we long for—emerges out of relationship, also the kind we long for.

We have been taught and have come to believe that an intimate relationship with another person is what will fulfill us, make us safe and happy, and give us what we most need. And perhaps that is true. But there is a deep—dare I say, deeper?—longing bred into each one of us, for contact with the beyond-human, with the realm of what every culture names "the Sacred." This becomes the task of religion and spiritual practices: to facilitate our connection with that "Other," however we might conceive of it. The forms of that central task are well known: prayer, chant, meditation, music, dance, mantra, and ritual. Each of these forms is fundamentally a mode of conversation—shape-shifting, ephemeral, undeniable, and usually indescribable. The two versions of what seems real, the two realms of body and spirit, attempt to bridge the vast gap between them. We know it happens. We know it is possible. We are surrounded by accounts from our ancestors and our neighbors. As fragmentary and partial as they might be (and they always are), each is a conversation.

There is a second great gap I try to navigate in this book, between the very abstract, even metaphysical Teachings from the Teachers, and the concrete practices recommended for us in our embodied, every day personal lives about how to walk this path of healing and awakening. I have found the resonance between those two levels, if you will, to be very instructive and helpful. Perhaps it will be for you as well.

So, what is this book about? The mysterious title, *The Radiant Heart of the Cosmos: Compassion Teachings for Our Time*, is meant to remind you of my previous book of Manjushri's Teachings: *What in the World Is Going On? Wisdom Teachings for Our Time*. There are many echoes between the two volumes, just as wisdom and compassion are always two views of a single reality in the Buddhist world.

The topics are simple, and the Teachings are clear and accessible. We are desperate for healing—as individuals, as families and communities, as a nation riven by mistrust and hatred, and as a planet reeling from our mindless destruction of our only home. We are overwhelmed by all we know now of ignorance, greed, and violence. And post-2020, we have had the plague, the Corona virus settling into every corner of human societies. We are swamped by fear, and rightly so.

To begin to extricate ourselves from this profound mess of our own making, we must begin by healing ourselves. We each must stop, listen within for the voices of fear and longing, and begin there. Our destination is the deep layers within, where old fears lie and fester. Even though they may be quite invisible, long forgotten, and long denied, they shape every aspect of our lives: who we are, how we relate, how we even see the world around us. Those hidden fears, buried in the Shadows of the unconscious, create what we believe is "the real world." It isn't, of course, for it is a world fashioned by illusions and projections. It is not a world where we might flourish.

In *What in the World Is Going On?* Manjushri teaches that we are in the midst of a vast Shower of Spirit, a Shower that reveals how our world is shaped by our fear. He invites us to wake up from our imagined fears. The reality of the Universe becomes visible when we walk this path of healing ourselves and then of our world. Even suffering and death can be held within this larger sense of reality. Manjushri invites each of us to take this journey. To wake up.

We begin by uncovering each fear that shapes our lives—recognizing it, respecting its vast power to conjure up imaginative stories, and breathing kindness to it. Slowly you will begin to realize that everyday thinking—cognitive mind, we might name it—seems to be running the show. It is playwright, producer, director, and even leading man or lady. We've caught a glimpse of little self, the constructed personality who lives in the world and protects its own identity. It is certain it knows who it is! Ha! says a deeper self, a deeper voice. Now, where did that come from? Who is that?

These questions form the rich core of this book and of a spiritual life centered on practices for accessing and opening the way to the heart center. Obscured for lifetimes by fears and denials and ignorance, buried under layers of scar tissue and defensive protections, the heart center within is a grand portal allowing access to that Reality of Many Names: Holy One, God, Allah, Source, Creator, Spirit, the Unnamable, the Infinite One, the Unknowable, the Eternal. Indeed, the Radiant Heart of the Cosmos. As you wish.

Portal is the key. Compassion, small c, is initially generated by a person's heart center and directed toward the wounded and the frightened. But Compassion, with a great C, pours through the portal of our newly revealed access to the cosmic Heart Center. This Compassion heals even as it stimulates vision, creativity, imagination, and generosity. It intends for life, even life only briefly in form, to flourish. It is the pulse, the breath of the Universe. It is, as you now might see, the Radiant Heart of the Cosmos.

We will move back and forth between the deeply personal and the more abstract, and we will hear the teaching voices of Manjushri and Kwan Yin, always embedded in conversational relationship with me. In Part I you will hear me speaking directly to you, for I wish to introduce myself and all my many hesitations and resistances to telling my story, so that you, dear Reader, might have a sense of who I am. At every step of writing this book, I have had you in mind, in the hope that what is here on the page will encourage and support you.

The Compassion Teachings in Part II reflect the metaphysical context within which the grand scheme begins to make some sense. Compassion is not just an ethical practice, fueled by the "should's" at the heart of so much religious teaching. It is, the Teachers argue, the core Reality of the cosmos. I have found that to be a profound and inexhaustible claim, which continues to challenge every piece of my conventional perceptions, assumptions, and knowledge.

The Teachings in Part III were given to me by both Manjushri and Kwan Yin in response to particular moments in my life, so they are more personal, informal, and strikingly conversational. They reflect the richness of our long relationships. I recognize their energies, and we have developed our own rhythms and patterns of conversation, as you will see.

I've chosen the topics for Part III because I think every seeker stumbles into these problems and wishes for some skillful ways to proceed. They are assuredly not in any particular order. In other words, don't get hung up on process! Poke around, find the essay that grabs your attention, and start there. Above all, be patient and willing to be surprised, even startled and challenged. Patience is necessary because the timing is not for you to choose. In fact, there is practically nothing for you to choose, except to continue your practice, honor your search, and welcome your slowly ripening devotion.

Part IV returns to the more abstract form of Teaching, with three pieces addressing directly what we face now, in our tumultuous world. Manjushri expands his Teaching on energy in the Shower of Spirit, and Kwan Yin and I send you off with encouragement for your long journey on the Spiral Path. Our hope, of course, is that your suffering will ease and your renewed vision into these tumultuous times will be full of insight and wisdom. May we all become more skillful, more open, and more creative as we join the challenging work of creating societies in which we would wish to live. In Part V, you will find four beloved teaching stories, which I have shared with countless students over the years. They remain sharp and provocative, in my mind, and just perfect for this deep work. And last, you will find the powerful Bodhisattva Prayer, chanted by the Dalai Lama and Buddhists all around the world.

One last note, to assist you as you read about heart and heart center. I try to distinguish as best I can between three versions of these terms; different languages and cultures understand the word "heart" to mean different things. Here, "heart" (lower case) will refer to the organ in your chest, which pumps blood. A person's non-physical organ of perception and feeling, located within the subtle bodies, is also "heart center," but in lower case. "Heart Center" (upper case) will refer to the portal for the source of compassion in the cosmos—indeed, the radiant heart of the cosmos.

Taylor

Part I

The Spiral Path

I invite you, dear Reader, to join me on this long and deeply human path, the Spiral Path, as it is so often named. I hope you will recognize yourself in the first short essay, "Who is This Book For?" and then be intrigued by what I describe in the second short essay, "What You Might Learn Here." Because I am inviting you to join a conversation with me and the Teachers, I will introduce myself as best I can, with plentiful descriptions of my hesitations and self-protective tactics and denials. In a way, that's a big part of the story. Certainly, those are the first territories requiring deep healing. So, sit down in a comfortable chair and allow me to tell you how this stunning experience came into my life, and what came with it!

Who Is This Book For and What Might You Learn?

Everyone I know suffers. Some suffer acutely, and some just go along with such chronic, low-level suffering they are hardly aware of it. Most would never use the word "suffering." And few would believe that relieving it is within their own power, their own heart and mind.

I hope that you may be able to begin to glimpse that underneath your discomfort and unhappiness lie deep patterns of self-protection against some potent, unknown fears. We rarely recognize that those self-protective practices actually deepen the discomfort and anxiety, as they are the "work" of that rather short-sighted aspect of ego I call "little self."

This book is for people who know themselves to be worn out and emotionally burdened, even though they have survived in an unwelcoming world. They know they have hidden so much of their inner reality that they have compromised their own integrity many times.

This book is for people who have been unable to settle comfortably within the religious tradition of their childhood, or of any other, for that matter.

This book is for people who like to think a lot, whose critical stance has protected them from so much foolishness, and for whom surrender to the unknowable is a very big ask—very, very big.

This book intends to be honest about how messy and challenging and just plain painful these inner and outer reckonings can be.

There are many accounts of sudden, instantaneous experiences of "waking up." According to those writers, there is a startling breakthrough, in just moments, after which nothing is ever the same again. I certainly don't doubt their accounts; but their advice to the rest of us is usually, "So don't be afraid!" Or, "Recognize universal Oneness!" Or....

For me, deep healing has required patient attentiveness, kindness, and self-understanding. Most of all, it has required surrender, over and over again. Deep "work," I must name it. This book is for those unable to simply call in the peak moment and the life-changing transformation as the old self dissolves.

From what I have learned, it seems that every bit of the person must be engaged—thinking, imagining, feeling, relating—and touched—body, mind, and soul. The long work of healing probes that small sense of self and profound dimensions of the unconscious. In the end, nothing is left out.

This book is for those whose karma or intuition or curiosity or desperation invites them into this greatest of all journeys. I will cheer you on, as I accompany you, step by step, through the simple gesture of handing you a book.

In the spirit of full disclosure, I must tell you that as I write these words, tears are running down my face and my body is shivering. I guess I've heard myself speak. Oh, dear Reader, here we go.

Here some crucial things that I have learned, to give you an overview of what you'll find as you read on in this book.

- A lot of suffering can be eased.
- Fear can be calmed down significantly.
- Old patterns within the self, some no longer helpful at all, can be identified and dismantled.
- New energies arrive, with new insights, new possibilities, new freedom, new creativity, new flexibility, and new visions.
- Wise assistance beyond measure is essential and available.
- A robust relationship with life-forming and heart-healing Spirit is available.
- This is a central reason to revisit the miseries of a life cramped by fears and taboos.

I follow here the pursuit of the most ancient wisdom, shared by all spiritual traditions. The gifts are healing, freedom, wholeness, and sanity, along with vastly expanded awareness or consciousness. And unless many of us begin to pursue these paths, our species may not survive. Everything, it seems, is at stake.

Penny's Story: The Story Behind the Stories

Most of us love to tell stories, whether they be hilarious or sad. We just plain love to talk, especially when we have the great gift of attentive listeners. I certainly do. Making a point via a story, or indulging in a little exaggeration in order to provoke laughter is simply delicious. Many of my former students would report that I often taught with stories. Storytelling is deeply human; it is how we place ourselves within the company of friends and kin.

There is another kind of story, a much deeper and more intimate story of who we really are, and how we came to be that person, as known from within. This story may never be told. The narrator of the story may not even know she holds this treasure in her very center. And when I say "treasure," please don't immediately assume I mean happiness and light. Not likely. It is more likely to be a tale of difficulties, challenges, obstacles, disappointments, and heartache. It is more likely to speak of the hard tasks of becoming a full and whole human being. It will probably carry tears in one hand and howls in the other.

To unearth this story is itself a great creative work. It requires heart-stopping courage and staggering perseverance. It will ask for form, which itself can demand years of disciplined apprenticeship. To recognize the arc of such a story may become so urgent that it bleeds into every part of a visibly normal life. Extruded, tempered, and compressed into linear time, it may also insist on adding older generations and other geographies, so the story is well grounded in its history.

But can the arc of a life—in its private inner meanderings—ever be stretched out in a straight line so as to settle into a row of sentences? Or is it too alive, too shimmering with invisible energies, and too vulnerable to the subtleties of mind and heart and spirit? Perhaps it is the case that the moment we truly know the arc of this story is the moment we take leave of our body, the moment we die.

It has been nearly impossible for me to tell this deep story of my life and how I came to be the person I most truly am. To write it, I had to wrestle for months, day after day, with mountains of resistance. This real story seemed so private, I didn't know if I was willing to bring it forth or how to do so.

When I began this new book, my plan was to introduce a series of Teachings on compassion. I would again take the role of student and scribe, as I had in *What in the World.* It seemed simple and straightforward, the perfect winter project.

But at every turn, I've been poked and prompted to include my own story of healing and transformation. My resistance has been fierce and dogged. I've been full of fear. I've raised countless objections and persuasive arguments on why this is not a good idea.

It hasn't worked. Step by step, I had to retreat and surrender. That deeply hidden central story will out. I don't know any other grammar to describe it better. That story, intimate and tender, completely private and shielded from the world's eyes, seems positively determined to be made visible to the world.

I meant to end there. But I've been sternly reminded I must add one more piece. I must say, I'm embarrassed that it had never occurred to me to include it. This will look like a postscript, but it actually sits at the very heart of my life story: I have suffered from acute and sustained health issues all my adult life.

This book is about healing and compassion, neither of which I would ever have thought about, much less longed for, when I was young. In my 30s, I was immersed in the tasks of a young adult: training for a career as a college professor, sorting out my central relationships, and situating myself in the adult world. In the midst of this, I was stricken with multiple attacks of acute pancreatitis. Each landed me in an intensive care unit for many days, and more than once I hovered between life and death. A diagnosis usually limited to old, alcoholic men, it made no sense to any of my physicians. Multiple surgeries over the next decade had no impact, and the devastating attacks continued. Eventually, as I became wiser about taking heed of early symptoms, it faded away, and my outer life continued on its trajectory.

A decade later, in my early 40s, I was stricken with a powerful neurological disease that stopped me cold. In the course of a week or two, I lost vast amounts of muscle strength and sensation. The fatigue was insurmountable. Within a couple of months, I had only two or three hours a day when I could function physically, i.e. teach a class or meet with a student. Otherwise, I lived on the sofa. It took a long time for a diagnosis: chronic inflammatory demyelinating polyneuropathy. A mouthful, yes; translating to an autoimmune function destroying the myelin sheathing around my peripheral nervous system. Though I'm much better now, the accommodations it requires remain a significant part of my life, nearly forty years later.

I share this history because each experience brought me to my knees, introducing me to my own vulnerability and to strange and frightening limits to my own well-being, forcing me to acknowledge and admit, "Yes, this is suffering. I need support and kindness." Prompted by these health challenges, the first lessons in surrender began to well up from within some unknown part of me. And with the first intimations of the practices of surrender came a mantra, unbidden, indeed, unrecognized as a mantra: "In Your hands. In Your hands." I had no idea what it meant or to whom it referred. It just murmured itself in the background. The path had opened and I was on my way. I didn't know that either, nor did I have any idea that I would be showered with compassion and healing, led by Teachers from "elsewhere" to the portal that is this book. I bow in endless gratitude—to the Teachers, the path, the book, and you, my readers.

The Deep Story

The real story, the deep story, the secret story, must be told from within. I don't know how to do that. By the very act of putting it into language, I have exited it. I am perched on the outside, peering down into the impenetrable darkness. What can I see? That's one problem. And what can I say? That is much harder. I see why there are poets and novelists. The poem need only point to something, and the reader is left to poke around between images and metaphors to see what she can discover. The writer of fiction invents a made-to-order character who will say whatever her maker intends. Again, the task of figuring out what is real and what is, well, less real, is left to the reader.

I'd like to save you that task. Or at the very least, I'd like to hold your hand while I point.

I could ask you, kindly, "Tell me, have you ever just been swamped by sadness? Sadness with no shape or texture?"

You would probably nod, sadly, for of course we all have.

And then I would say, "Ah, lean into that sadness, hold it against your chest or find where it lives in your body. Touch it gently on the arm. That is the doorway to your shining heart, and that is the way to your healing."

That is the entrance to the Spiral Path of healing, of infinite compassion, of profound clarity about the human condition, as the old scholars named it. I can't tell you what you will discover on your path, for it is the exquisite display of all your unlived life, of betrayal and disappointment, of loss and rage, of unwept tears and stony silences. It holds all the moments when, in your distress, you turned your back on life.

"Go," I say, "go! I send you off with blessings, with courage and curiosity and infinite patience. All the rest will be given to you."

"Who are you?" you ask. "How do you know these things? And why do you say so little?"

"I know these things because I have lived them, for years and perhaps for lives. Who knows? And who am I? Well, not the person I appear to be. There is some other center within, which is more truly who I am. She is what remains after hundreds of accrued bits and pieces gathered over my long life have fallen away. I can't name her, and so, there we are. And why do I say so little? Oh, I ache to say more, truly, but I cannot find the words. I'm doing my best, right now. I am a mystery to myself, for sure, so of course I am also a mystery to you."

This is one teaching of the Spiral Path: that you are most certainly not who you have thought you were, and you won't be who you really are, until you don't know!

You are quite right: I sound like the Cheshire Cat trying to explain something to Alice. I can't help it.

The way is long and hard, full of turns and repeats and dead ends.

I have stumbled over griefs like potholes in the road. I learned I could cry, and then, day after day, I allowed yet another long-gone moment to drain itself of its tears. There was a 50-year backlog of unwept tears to work through. Those blessed tears cleared out so much toxicity as well as old rigidities frozen in place. The path behind me lay littered with cast-off memories and grievances and betrayals.

I was gaining skills, as I plodded along, as well. The patterns were so familiar. I was astonished, and then irritated. Really? Haven't I wrestled with that memory many times already? Again and yet again? At least I no longer erected another row of bricks on the wall of resistance. I learned it was better to ask what purpose that pattern had served for my vulnerable younger self. To ask: Is it still necessary or even appropriate for me now? Not likely. Breathe some gratitude to it for its service years ago, and then give that younger self a warm hug, and continue on your way. A remarkable new strategy, if I may call it that, which continues to ease my life.

Further down that relentless spiral, I stumbled upon the ancient wound, which I came to name the core task of my life. My curriculum. My twin companion, the loneliness woven into every inch of the fabric of my life and who I became. The loneliness was wedded to the most human of fears, and it has lived in me in many guises: the infant's need to be welcomed into her parent's care; the unvoiced threats of abandonment by absent parents; the casual refusals to recognize a child's complexity; and the clear message, year after year, I was simply too "different" to be easily brought into the shelter of kin and companions. My visible life, my life visible to others, was carefully curated. All the rest was stashed out of view—sometimes knowingly and sometimes straight into the unconscious.

I actually don't think I was so different after all. Probably most of us—certainly those of us robustly socialized into the brittle and demanding society of the post-war United States, empire in all but name—have lived these tragically corseted lives. But I was blessed with the rare good fortune of being broken open early in my adult life. I was brought to my knees with devastating illness, several times vanishing into a coma and starting to take leave. I was just 30. That kind of suffering shook me to my roots; it was an unmistakable wake-up call to figure out what was happening to me and why.

I've been on this journey now for nearly 50 years. Maybe it is time for me to admit to myself that this has actually been the purpose and meaning of this life. One might point to karma, of course, and one might name it my vocation. It has surely been my quest, usually framed as my persistent desire to understand the huge questions: what is life for? Is there more to reality than what we can see and measure? Is there meaning to be discovered, or must we settle for having told oneself a good story? How can we know what really matters, if anything really does?

I will tell more stories as we go along, that you may chuckle in recognition and to encourage you when you are weary and discouraged. Keep fear and loneliness in mind, please, for they are literally the touchstones of human suffering and human healing into freedom. As the Dalai Lama reminds us so often, may he be blessed, "It is a profound and rare gift to have a human life!"

Fear and Resistance

My main inner work of late has been to slowly dismantle the mountain of resistance to sharing this story. It is partly a long practice of privacy, honed during my nearly fifty years in a college classroom, where so much of the teacher's personal life must remain invisible, in order to protect the space for the students. I quite agree that the personal is political, but it is not always pedagogically appropriate.

That was my first line of argument, but the real source of the resistance was much older and more firmly rooted in the foundation of who I am. I was certain that to reveal my inner life—intellectual, emotional, and spiritual—would be extremely dangerous.

Let me say that again, because it is so weird, really, that I thought it true. I was taught, as a child, "Don't let anyone know how smart you are, or no one will like you." I was taught that to express a difficult feeling, like sadness or anger, would lead to rejection and abandonment. That the only way to be liked, included, and cared for was to be unfailingly cheerful, cooperative, and kind. That this was the instruction for me in a rather unwelcoming second family lent it a lot of credibility.

Let me skip forward now, from grade school to graduate school, where I suddenly and very unexpectedly discovered that as a young woman at Yale I was a barely tolerated presence in the most male-dominated environment I had ever encountered. In seminars my questions and comments were ignored. Now I can see that I was simply too "outside the box" for those self-assured men, but then I interpreted it to mean that I wasn't going to be a successful academic. I said less and less about the matters at hand, except with a few classmates over weekend dinners.

Much of that intellectual silencing was relieved by a long career teaching wonderful students at a superb women's liberal arts college. At Mount Holyoke, I landed in the perfect place to teach and learn. But still I was extremely careful not to speak of my inner life, given the taboos so fiercely enforced in the academic world.

These were the mental and emotional habits of mind that I brought to my first encounters with the Teachers. Those habits had so shaped me that I was almost unaware of them. The filters worked automatically. There was no need to be intentional about my constant, meticulous self-silencing and self-editing. My whole identity—as a faculty member, later dean of the college, and a person intensely interested in politics and the great reform movements of my generation—depended on my inner life's invisibility.

The Teachers Arrive

I was about 60 when this uneasy equilibrium was disturbed by the other realm, which is how I have named it—some space of reality beyond the everyday, three-dimensional world confirmed constantly by our five senses.

My first encounter with a Teacher not in body was with Kwan Yin, the great Deity of compassion—"She who hears the cries of the world," especially beloved among Buddhists in East and Southeast Asia. She is also, I would later learn, a female manifestation of Avalokiteshvara, the central bodhisattva of the Himalayan Buddhist world. The Dalai Lama is understood to be a reincarnation of that beloved Deity of wisdom and compassion. I knew none of that at the time. I was just driving along a lovely country road in western Massachusetts, weary beyond measure, sad, and stuck in patterns that were causing me ever more suffering and loneliness. I was on my way to my weekly Pilates lesson, which was usually frustrating, but the slow stretching always helped me relax and settle.

Suddenly, I heard myself cry out, in the car, alone, "Kwan Yin, why won't you help?" And immediately, a clear response: "Oh, we thought you would never call." Shaking, I pulled over to the side of the road and tried to steady myself. I had an idea who Kwan Yin was, in a vague sort of way. A good friend had multiple statues and images of her around her house, and I had rather disinterestedly admired them. As my breathing slowed down, I drove on to my Pilates class, deeply perplexed. I didn't know where my cry had come from, for it was entirely spontaneous and utterly bewildering. It would signal my eventual opening to a new life and a new understanding of a full human life.

I had been a journal writer for many years, a practice that I had begun in my 30s, as a way to record and work with dreams. I had met a remarkable Jungian therapist in London, who taught me about dreams and how to harvest their rich gifts. That will belong in another story. It arises now because Kwan Yin and I eventually would meet in my journal every morning, as we do to this day. Our morning conversation and/or Teaching would become my central spiritual practice, though I surely did not know that in those early days. She was my wise adviser on how to navigate my extremely complicated personal and professional life. There was so much I needed to learn about how buried parts of me were directing so much of my life, my relationships, my decisions, and even my hopes for myself. Sometimes she pointed to an aspect of a dream. Sometimes she noted how I was seriously misreading someone else's intentions. Sometimes she insisted I get more rest and take better care of myself, rather than pouring out energy to others, day and night. I think I received some stunning re-parenting, frankly, in how to live a more sane and balanced life.

Manjushri's arrival was just as unexpected. I had arrived at my beloved island cabin in Lake Superior in mid-June, after an exhausting semester. Morning after morning I tried to put it all down into my journal, so that I might be free to enjoy the gifts of my summer world. I poured out my distress about climate change, American adventurism in the Middle East, and the cascading problems of neo-liberal globalization. Hunger and poverty were rampant in the wealthiest country in the world, as we surrendered to the domination of unregulated markets. Page after page of despair.

One morning, a clear strong voice said calmly to me: "That's not how we see it!" I would learn, in the next days and weeks, that this was the voice of Manjushri, the most prominent manifestation of wisdom in the Himalayan Buddhist world. He offered to explain to me their view of things, and I agreed.

Thus began my apprenticeship to the Teachers, which would become my introduction to a new life shaped by the support, the instruction, and then the call to live in alignment with Spirit.

Inner Transformation

The first visible fruit of my encounters with the Teachers was my 2015 book of Teachings from Manjushri, *What in the World Is Going On? Wisdom Teachings for Our Time*. The invisible fruit, however, was also being cultivated. Profound inner transformation was underway, and that is the theme of this book.

To speak at all of this long process is hard for me; to describe it clearly is impossible. That's not hard to understand, for much went on at a very deep level of my interior self. And the observing self—me, who I mostly think I am—was also shape-shifting, so that both the knower and the known were unstable, if not unreliable. And who was able to critique and judge? Even simple conventions of subject/object began to melt away.

Everything I have said so far is true and did happen. But it is not the whole truth. In court, one must swear "to tell the truth, the whole truth, and nothing but the truth," which is a high standard. I must try to bear witness to the truth of who I am, my story and my journey. The whole truth is simple. My life was drenched with fear and loneliness and shame. Spirit knocked and knocked on the door to my heart, but my heart had long been shut down and buried. Most of me was not home, and there was no one to answer the knocking.

I have said before, the universe intends for us to flourish. I was certainly not flourishing. I was hanging on and pushing through, doing my work as best as I knew how. Sometimes for days or even months, it felt like a weary forced march, with no obvious destination except to keep moving. That was not depression, not in any clinical sense. I was living a responsible, successful, and respected life in this particular cultural moment when such inner poverty is so easily dismissed.

Perhaps I had to tell this story because my life—the suffering, the inner hungers and isolation, the loneliness and shame, the thin gruel that passed for meaningfulness—was so normal. It is probably no exaggeration to say that the fact that I was able to respond to the knocking was the greatest blessing of my life, even though it would inaugurate years and years of painful self-discovery.

So begins the story of the Spiral Path into the depths, the path of discovery, healing, and compassion.

Bearing Witness to My Journey: Five Stories

I suspect I could tell a lot of my life history just by pointing out all the moments when there was a dance between a call and a hesitation, an opportunity and a fear. Manjushri said recently, half laughing at me: "No whining!"

I offer five stories here, partly for your amusement and partly because I'm hoping they might resonate with your experience too.

Not Me! I'm Just a Regular Person!

Most of us can name a mystic or two. Some of us are familiar with many. We have found deep comfort in the works of mystics from every religious tradition, if by mystic we mean someone who claims or is known by others to have access to an other-worldly, non-earthly realm. The mystic may share some of what she receives as writings, ecstatic speech, art, music, dance or ritual. If we include the shamanic practices of indigenous societies, we would want to note physical and mental healing for both individuals and communities. Some mystics remove themselves from society and retreat to a hidden life. Some hide in full view in monasteries or families, hospitals or schools, and never reveal their quietly secret lives. I would guess we meet mystics rather more often than most of us realize.

Still, if we think about it, we hold an image of a mystic as someone who lived centuries ago, probably on another continent; who practiced serious austerities, maybe not bathing very often; someone we definitely would not invite home for dinner. We are fascinated by what they have left us: letters, sermons, teachings recorded by students, and commentaries on sacred texts. We trust their accounts, slender as they may be, because we recognize how they surrendered their lives, whole and entire, to their relationship with the divine, with the Holy Other.

That they really existed, lived lives in particular places at particular times, and wrote books we still read and find valuable, is a profound comfort. We are reassured, perhaps, there is more to life than our daily round, welcome or challenging as it may be.

I count myself among the most appreciative that they lived, and that some at least left us accounts of their lives in the presence of the Sacred. Something in me goes on alert when I meet a new text or discover a hermit meditator who left us some teaching. But "alert" doesn't mean quick acceptance. No, I search for clues of the depth and authenticity of a mystic text. Is it robust enough for me to trust that it emerged out of long struggle and devoted practice? Is it embedded in a rich tradition or lineage? I try to exercise my best skills of discernment, but in the end, I probably rely largely on a "gut feeling" I might or might not have.

I'm not alone with this problem of discerning authenticity. Religious authorities have their criteria. One is usually "does this support our community's beliefs and practices?" I like the measure in the Christian stories about saints: Judge the claims by the behavior of the claimant. But even that is tricky, because the post-mortem stories raise their own interpretive problems.

I write all this, because it points to yet another of my persistent, grudging hesitations, which I believe I must confess here. People like me ("regular people," as a friend described me recently; "a person who wears woolen sweaters and down vests") don't become mystics. For sure, that's true. Isn't it? Whew. That's a relief. Got that taken care of. So now can I continue to live my "regular life" in my sweater and down vest, and remain hidden, not only to the world, but also to myself? That's the plan, isn't it?

Trying to write this book and these short essays has blocked all the exits. I simply must put down these veils, composed half of denial and half of cowardice. My Soul is collapsing with laughter right now. I have never once said to myself or out loud to anyone else: I am a mystic. Though surely I am. There, I've said it. I've written it down. *I am a mystic.* Great Teachers from another realm have leaned into my world and spoken life-changing Teachings to me. It simply is what has happened, as best as I can report it. I'm a mystic.

Fear of Failure

Oh, Manjushri Sir, I had planned to ask you for help today with the new book: for a plan, for suggestions, for help with focus and direction. Instead, I arrive now full of tears, shaking with fear about this project. It is too hard, too complicated, and way beyond my skill and experience. I have no idea what I'm doing, what I might be doing, or how to proceed. I have no confidence whatsoever. I just can't do this. It is too much, too much. And I can't stop sobbing. It is too hard. I don't have the vision or confidence or energy. I'm too old, too weary, too worn out, and too much on my own. I just can't prop myself up any more.

Oh, dear Pennyla. The weeping is helpful, and recognizing the fear is very helpful. Do not interrupt either. Let them flow through you. Sit quietly now, drink your tea, and breathe kindness to your very weary self. We will speak a little later.

OK. Thank you. I'm hoping we can try again.

Yes. We must address the fear. And then, we will begin to outline a plan for your work, and how we will proceed. This is not your book; this is our book. This is very important. You offer to do this because you wish to respond to our call to you and to share the Teachings with others. You already share our Teachings, seamlessly and unselfconsciously, when you speak. It shows how deeply you have integrated them into your understanding of how to live a good and meaningful life. Now you recognize, in part because of the responses to your new website, that the Teachings must be put into a form that facilitates their move out into the world. Even more than *What in the World*, this will ripple out in ways you cannot imagine.

The fear, as you named it, is the fear of failure. You are not well acquainted with that, and it shocked you. There is no harm in that. But this will not fail. It cannot, unless you decide to withdraw. We consider that unlikely, but the taste of that fear is in your mouth, and it still rumbles in your belly. Your subtle bodies contracted, as they do in the face of a flood of fear. The slow cup of tea allows that clench to release.

You need only two words: surrender and trust. You must let go of your very muscular sense of responsibility for this project. You must recognize that we will guide you, step by step, until you can see your way. We know what we are doing and what we are asking of you! Trust that as well, please.

You also fear dying before this work is completed. In one sense, of course, you will die before the work is completed. You are deeply skilled at our collaborative work, and it will continue for many years. But there is no obvious end point, so it may well be incomplete when you leave this Earth.

There is no harm in that. Others do this work, and others have done it, and will do it. There are always teachers, and there are always Beings who tend and instruct them. It is how human life has always worked and will continue to work. Rejoice that you have found yourself within the great stream of those who welcome the guidance and instruction from those Teachers not in body. When they can share what they have been given, it is enough. Truly, it is enough.

Today, finish the fall chores and start a good book, please. Listen to music. Help the new rhythm emerge, so it can support you. This will proceed beautifully, beloved student and partner. Remember: Surrender and trust.

Doubts

Writing this book has revealed so much resistance, I really thought it would never cease. It was a miserable process to identify such deeply rooted fear. Resistance to allowing myself to be seen. Resistance to the hard labor of uncovering the story and shaping it into something helpful and accurate. Resistance to feeling and revealing my vulnerabilities, which turned out to be legion.

And the fears—the fear of failure, of course, but also, more surprisingly, the fear of success. Beyond the fear of not being useful to you, my reader, there was also the fear of ego getting all puffed up and ridiculous. Fear of ego belittling me, judging me, and criticizing my self-absorption.

These, however, are little fears, more like the stinging black flies that hover around my head in June. I'm not in the mood today to try to distinguish among fears, resistances, doubts, and hesitancies. They are countless and relentless and always present whether I acknowledge them or pretend I've managed to pull out ahead of them. They rise up out of some deeper, perhaps primordial, level.

I've mentioned how these fears of self-exposure or self-revelation reflect a deep anxiety that was instilled in me as a child, when I understood that to be seen truthfully would endanger my acceptance by my family, my peers, and my world. Beneath that crouched the ever-present fear of abandonment, and, since we are herd animals, the danger of death. We all know this. To be safe, one must belong; to belong, one must conform to the shared model of an acceptable human life. It is likely rooted in our neurology. Those stinging black flies of fear remind us of this and push us back into the mainstream of our world. Back into the herd where we belong.

Here is the real dread: What if nothing is real? What if nothing matters? What if there is no meaning in a human life, not even in music or philosophy, ceremony or physics, love or generosity? What if our elaborate narratives about human life, about life itself, are simply our doodles in the long sand beaches of our lives?

It's not just that our small brains don't have the capacity to answer these questions, although that is probably the case. But the questions themselves trigger a great cosmic yawn; nope, there is nothing here for you. It all began as random chemical processes ignited by a very great explosion into matter, and we must admit eventually it is the source of all that is, including us.

It is a very bracing view.

I would guess many humans stumble into this featureless void, though probably few seek it out. If you'd like a taste of it, go out on a clear night and lie down on the grass. Let your gaze move from horizon to horizon, and remind yourself about stars and galaxies, about distances and speeds we cannot grasp, and breathe through that crescendo of awareness. Remind yourself of your size and years.

As I said, it is a very bracing view.

And now I'm to tell you that two Beings not in body, apparently not even bound by time and space, speak to me and care that I find ways to share what they have to say with others? I'm to write with a clear voice of my own, that yes, this has been my experience, and here are their Teachings, as best I could grasp them? I'm to tell you that their views are helpful? That these Teachings matter?

Truly, it is not that I fear your doubt or mockery. That you are reading this suggests you might be a sympathetic companion. No, I fear that this long hard work of many years, with its weeping and heart ache, is nothing more than a child's cross-stitch on a dish towel, a place to exercise a certain focus and discipline. An opportunity for me to engage with a complicated text, which continues to reveal parts of me that I had long ago stashed away into the darkness of memory. And with good reason.

I've chosen to hold open this view and not to shut it down and lock it away because the tension is so unpleasant. I've chosen to embrace with my whole heart and mind—well, most of it—that the very nature of reality is kindness, is love, and that what comes into form is meant to flourish. I've chosen to agree that there is meaning here and that our purpose, while in form, is to attend to the flourishing of ourselves and each other. I've learned these many years that healing and ease can emerge, as well as a wide and spacious mind, a mind awakened to what is, and therefore full of wonder and awe.

I was told that I must bear witness to who I am. This is all I can say.

Whose Voice?

This is the hardest question of all. What are these voices, where do they come from, and really, whose are they? Where am *I* in this flood of language and wisdom? And how does this happen?

I have been asked these questions countless times, especially at readings and talks. I have no good answers to any of them. All I can do is describe the experience as best I can. Kwan Yin appeared about twenty years ago, and Manjushri joined her about five years later. Their voices—inner and not audible to normal hearing—are easy to distinguish. Hers is kind and usually gentle. Her insights into people are brilliant, as is her support for my healing and waking up. Manjushri teaches, and that word should probably be in bold print. His voice is unmistakably authoritative, stunning in its precision and clarity, and nearly impersonal. I've never doubted that one is female and the other male. From the tone and rhythm, I learned to gauge and distinguish their energies.

And their origin? Ah, truly an impossible question, though each would say some version of "Well, the Teachers speak to their students from a different realm." I wondered for many years about their possible connection with what we call "archetype" or Jung's concept of the collective unconscious. Is there some boundary where a person's psyche intersects with some transcendent psychic energy or another dimension? It seems likely to me, but who knows? And how could we know it, moreover?

One thing is absolutely clear to me: there are Teachings and insights, sentences and observations, which are so startling, so entirely beyond anything I could possibly think or create or imagine (and truly, I'm not shy about any of that), that the material must come from elsewhere—way beyond the reach of my own intellect and consciousness.

I've had to allow the questions to rest in that space of mystery, of what cannot be known by a human mind. Their voices have remained distinct from each other, and from mine. For someone who had spent her life in the world of the academy, with its epistemological assumptions and taboos, it was already a lot to live with. A lot.

The Teachings continued to arrive, and I eventually published Manjushri's book. It was well received by many readers, even deeply skeptical ones. I got used to their questions about that channeled voice, and I would only be able to say, "Really, I have no idea. It is just how it happens." I had to leave the questioner to wrestle with it herself, if she wished.

And then, it began to change. The voices began to merge. At first the voices of Manjushri and Kwan Yin became less distinct, though I can still tell which is which, most of the time. But then my voice began to resemble the Teachers' voices. And what was more disturbing was that readers, friends, and a wise editor reported the same confusion. One said to me, "It seems as if you, Penny, are hiding behind Manjushri when you quote him or present a Teaching." Mostly I chose to ignore the evidence, because the implications terrified me.

As I've worked on this new book, these questions have gotten more pressing. How shall I mark the three voices, especially in the chapters originally from the 2004 – 2013 manuscript of *The Compassion Teachings*? Or the selections from the Teachings of both Manjushri and Kwan Yin, found in Part III? They are selected from texts received over nearly two decades, from 2004 to 2021. It was becoming a great jumble, while the life-long teacher and scholar in me kept trying to pin down source and date for each passage. As you will see, I've noted the source for each Teaching, but not its date, as there is nothing chronologically significant about when I received the Teachings. Many were repeated over and over, until I was finally able to absorb them.

For a while I considered putting each of the three voices in a different font, to make it easy to recognize who was saying what. But that didn't solve the question about how the voices were becoming ever more similar with each other. And there was another fraught implication: if our voices were merging, were we merging? Voice expresses the essence of a person, doesn't it? The very timbre and rhythm of language, even if indefinable, seem essentially individual, perhaps even unique.

Well, I thought, during the long days of Covid solitude, perhaps I'm so immersed in their Teachings that I'm absorbing their language. Perhaps, even simpler, it is an artifact of that subtle process of my "translating" their messages into language—hopefully into legible English. But that has been our process for twenty years. What is different now?

Perhaps the years of relationship with each of them, the long and intense path of inner clarification and healing, and of discovering how ungrounded so many of the firm beliefs of the conscious self are, have led to this strange phenomenon. I no longer trust my old, powerful conviction that the self is stable and long-lasting, with clear boundaries between self and other. Maybe we all are receiving impulses and insights from what would seem to lie beyond the conscious self; or maybe at least we all have that capacity, if we were open to it?

I don't know. And again, I don't know how I can know. These are circular problems, where knower and known are tightly intertwined. As I said, if the distinctions between self and other blur, then the distinctions between subject and object also blur. Who knows, and who is known? I don't know. However, I do notice that it only troubles that former way of understanding myself, "former" meaning before engaging with the Teachers, many years ago. I will leave it at that, in the surround of mystery.

So, dear Reader, please know this: The text you hold in your hand reflects all three voices—Kwan Yin's, Manjushri's, and mine. The Teachings, with their great breadth and depth and power, are theirs. And that is what matters.

Shining

"Don't ever let people know how bright you are, or they won't like you." I don't know when my mother first warned me of this. Perhaps it became part of the family furnishings when she married again, when I was four. She was a war widow, as my father had been killed in World War II; I was a war orphan, I suppose. The new family offered complicated terrain for my young self, including the strange, unspoken calculation that this girl child must not challenge or embarrass her new stepfather.

But the advice from Mother was also about living in the wide world; it was meant to help me protect myself in a society that didn't approve of smart women, including my mother. She taught kindergarten for a few years when I was little, and then exited paid work. She would have been a superb school principal; our town—like towns all over the country—lost out in its eagerness to reestablish the primacy of men in the post-war American labor force.

Is it possible to teach a child self-denying behaviors in order to protect her from public dangers? Yes, of course. Today we watch Black parents instructing their sons how not to trigger a white policeman. But Mother's warning about not being liked, not being part of the peer group, and not having friends belonged to another universe compared to one where a simple gesture by a middle school kid could get him shot, point blank.

I don't remember worrying about not having school friends, and I doubt I ever argued with her about her fears. I'm guessing I got the message, and took appropriate care not to "stick out," for kids really don't like that, for sure. And certainly not from girls.

But it crippled something in me, something strong and potent, full of energy and joy. I didn't fully understand this until I retired, at least 60 years since the first instruction. By then, of course, it had shaped me and my life.

I have learned these last years how I took that motherly advice in, adding layers of self- protection over my quick intelligence, intuitive insight and irreverent speech, which would mock someone's self-importance.

My tender heart, so rooted in the nameless realm of Spirit, also had to be buried and carefully hidden, lest it upset the various local principalities of school, college and graduate school. My apprenticeship in the world of the university and its many ways of refusing me entrance, respect, and true intellectual and creative freedom would require a longer essay. You can see, I am sure, how that would have reinforced the family patterns, which required self-silencing and self-censorship. I practiced the disciplines of hiding myself as if my life depended upon it. I believed it did.

All of this is true, as best as I can remember. But it is not yet the whole story. Something lies deeper than this.

Towards the end of her long life, when there had been much healing and easy affection between us, I asked Mother two questions that had long bothered me.

"You have so often spoken of your worries about my brother and sister. Why have you never worried about me? And why did you so rarely acknowledge or praise an accomplishment of mine?"

She laughed at the first one: "Oh, Honey, why would I ever worry about you? I always knew, you could solve any problem you faced!"

But the second question brought a different tone and a sudden wrench of sadness. "Oh, dear Penny, when you were little, you would just shine! The shining would break through so powerfully; it was stunning. I had to turn away, sad because I couldn't share it with Tom [my birth father]. It was too painful, and I had to turn away."

Tears come, as I write this. Nearly as old as she was then, I weep for her and her unhealed grief. And I weep for myself, with my own unhealed loss and grief. Did her turning away shape me in some way? I have no idea. But there is that word, "shining." I think that might be the clue I'm looking for.

What shines in a young child's face when she is still in her wholeness, is that lively presence of Spirit, full of light and trust. It is why we so love children. Their transparency probably has evolutionary value, for it draws us to care for them in their total vulnerability.

Gradually or rapidly, the child's light dims. Perhaps it is shrouded under all that must be learned and mastered. Some societies are able to recognize a child's inner spirit, arranging support and teachings so she might bring her gift to the whole community. But it was not so in my family or our little world, which valued practical skills, common sense, and fitting in.

I think I usually knew that the flickering light was still there. I searched out nourishment: time outdoors, camping, campfires, Girl Scout activities and nature study were wonderful. I collected inspirational poems and secretly read the whole Bible when I was about ten. I can see now how I tried to find my way into the vast world of Spirit, though there was no sign of it in my family or school. It was my private business and no one else's.

And so, from my grade school years onward, I shaped a life in which that deep inner reality was never absent, even as it was absolutely private. Were there still moments of "shining"? Probably. There would have been some sweet leakage from time to time, when I gave a talk or helped a friend figure out something complicated in her life.

It was only when it came time to publish the Manjushri Teachings, in 2015, that I had to come out of that life-long enclosure, erected to protect my inner privacy. Slowly, oh, so slowly, in the years since, that enclosure has been dissolving. Preaching occasional sermons stripped some armor away. Creating a website and posting on my blog opened up another chink or two. Same with Facebook posts, and long emails to former students. And when I moved to the island to begin a new life in a very different kind of community, well, there was no turning back. I was no longer in charge of that intricate self-hiding. I suspect that some islanders know I'm a little different, and yet also trustworthy in a way that is hard to name. I'm profoundly grateful. Their easy, warm welcome has given me new life and new freedom. They don't even seem to mind that sometimes the shining leaks out. It has been deeply healing.

This is what I've learned: There is nothing *but* Shining!

Part II

The Compassion Teachings

Teachings from Manjushri

Introduction

I had a memorable conversation with a very wise elder, one afternoon when I was in my early 30s. She asked me how I felt about such-and-such. I responded easily, "Oh, what I think is...."

"No, no," she insisted. "Not what you *think*. What do you *feel*?"

I had no idea. I doubt that I even realized that one could indeed *feel* something, rather than think about it. She seemed shocked. I was just puzzled.

Thus began my long, long search to uncover my feelings. If I had known how demanding that search would be, I probably would have balked. Fortunately, I didn't. In a way, this book is both a testament to and a map of that long path from a silenced and buried emotional life to a late-life immersion in the wonders of compassion, both human and divine. On the way, I had to uncover the long-ignored feelings, welcome a more heart-centered life, and then, astonished, discover the Heart Center and how it is a portal for the grand energies of kindness and compassion from the other realm.

Another way to describe that long journey is to say that I had to recover my relationship with the feminine, both in my own heart and in its divine form. Because so much of what ails our world is the consequence of the ancient suppression of the Divine Feminine, source of compassion, healing, and fertility, my journey is a micro-version of what our civilization must also do. These Teachings, then, can be read on both levels—the personal and the planetary.

I could not have traversed this path without the guidance of the Teachers. You have already heard a bit about that in the pages above: Kwan Yin's morning Teachings, and how the kindness of her attentive energy slowly melted some of the barricades within me. Later,

Manjushri's extraordinary Teachings on fear pulled up to the surface life-long structures in my very person, which had shaped me from head to toe. To disentangle all that took years, even with careful, step-by-step instructions.

But decades into this slow process, I still would never have used the words "healing" or "energy." I don't know how else to tell you how ignorant I was of how to live a fully human life. I had no idea I needed healing, much less how much or how deeply. Healing is what people needed if they were ill, traumatized, or addicted. Not me, for heaven's sake! And I would have cringed before the suggestion that a little compassion for my own suffering would be good medicine. Me, need compassion? Me, suffering? Not a chance.

I loved Manjushri's Teachings on fear, which so elegantly analyzed the human condition and the state of the world. That I could understand. Publishing *What in the World* filled me with trepidation, but a lot of quiet joy as well.

But I was startled when Manjushri offered another set of Teachings on compassion, at just about the same time *What in the World* came out. After that, the Compassion Teachings lay hidden in plain sight on my computer for six years. I had a lot to learn, before they would ring deeply true for me.

One of the many gifts of retirement has been that work is no longer available for self-soothing or self-medicating, as folks say. Sudden insights about long-ignored aspects of my life burst into view in the spaciousness of my new life. It was awful. Painful. Full of tears and then anger and then tears again.

If you don't recognize you need healing, you will not be searching for compassion, either. In fact, you might not even be receptive to compassion. That's a bit of a puzzle. When healing seems urgently necessary, it feels like a catastrophic defeat. That little self who prides itself on its self-sufficiency and autonomy is allergic to admitting it desperately needs both healing and compassion. Losing control of events or recognizing one's own powerlessness to arrange your life as you wish can overcome the habitual refusal to ask for help, on both the individual and the collective levels. The values of autonomy and self-reliance are knit into the sinews of American society and culture. If you want evidence, take a long look at what Covid revealed about the so-called "safety net" for Americans facing one catastrophe after another. We have done this to ourselves.

Compassion can arrive from three directions. It can come from a kindly encounter with a person who sees our suffering and need, and responds. Secondly, you can wrap yourself in compassion. That may sound weird, but I've learned that it is as simple as can be. Watch a young child suck her thumb or reach for her teddy bear. She is giving herself comfort and treating herself with compassion. And she can, marvelous to tell, because she has not yet developed an inner voice telling her it is foolish or self-indulgent. The third source of compassion is what I call "the other realm," the energy of the cosmos in its endless forms, which can enact healing through compassion.

I have learned that simply breathing out kindness to myself for three or four exhales can begin the calming I so clearly need in the moment. By witnessing myself and acknowledging that I'm having a tough moment, I can lessen my distress. Please, if this sounds absurd, just try it. It is amazingly effective. The conscious witness and the kindly response shift the energy. It is an essential practice of compassion for self and other, which initiates long-term processes of healing. It also, almost as a bonus, erodes the resistance of that stubborn little self to dissolving its old patterns of denial and defensiveness.

We live in a fractal universe, where the micro and the macro are often intimately related. We can shift our focus from the tiniest micro level—that's me—to the vastest conceptual level imaginable. Manjushri speaks metaphysically of the ceaseless pulse in the universe, of energy moving into form and then out of form. While in form, beings intend to stay in form. Yet they do not—indeed, they cannot, and this causes suffering. Because moving into and out of form is the fundamental nature of the universe, suffering and the desire to avoid suffering reveal themselves to be a core feature of reality. And so, we must start with that firmly in mind.

The other core feature of reality is that the universe "intends" (a tricky word here) for life in form to flourish. The desire to flourish, shared by all forms of life, is another way to describe the suffering inherent in reality.

The universe's response to that suffering is compassion. Or, you might shift your view a little and say that compassion and suffering are two aspects of a single energetic process.

In the powerful Teachings that follow, the complex polarity of feminine and masculine will be discussed, and how that duality has become the lens to understand many aspects of human life. We will meet Noah's wife, and be shown more of what has been lost by the silencing of the feminine. We will see hints of how what we loosely name "the Divine Feminine" in the invisible realms, that basic pulse of the universe, is the source of Compassion. Capital C Compassion. Reminded of the staggering imbalances in our social and global lives between the masculine and the feminine, with their different emotional and mental habits, we will be told (but of course we already know) that our very survival as a species depends upon our ability to welcome the feminine—both divine and human—back into the very center of our lives.

And so we arrive at the necessity of healing. We must heal ourselves before we can heal our communities and our world. As our own hearts address the fears that undergird our lives, we begin to gain access to the Heart Center, the source of the profound cosmic pulse of Compassion.

What needs to be healed? And how do we learn to identify that? I think now, after a lot of tearful messing about in these emotional spaces, that we must be healed of our fears. Our fears are legion, for sure, and they shape-shift and cluster and rise up unexpectedly. More than anything else, they shrink us into tiny, claustrophobic lives. We express less than a handful of who we are, and even that, with caution.

Peer under any simple fear, and see what lies below. Repeat, over and over. Grieve and mourn and rage at how those fears were deposited into your child heart. Then look again. Eventually, we arrive at the fear we share with all sentient beings: our fear of death. Of becoming prey for a predator—whether a tiger, much larger than we are, or a tiny but no less deadly virus.

And where might you discover a flash of compassion? In that early morning darkness, with a fresh cup of coffee and candles lit. In the swirling warmth of a grand "wink" from a beloved elder. In the vast expanse of the Great Lake, ready to receive your lament without complaint. In the sharp clarity of a sentence that comes to you "out of nowhere," strangely reflecting the Sword of Discernment. In the deep, dark eyes of your dog looking at you, understanding without words what your heart is saying to her. The perfect call from the perfect friend at the perfect moment. Slowly, oh, ever so slowly, you begin to see that all the dots are connected. The universe breathes compassion; like a great cosmic eye, it witnesses sorrow and sends out compassion.

Manjushri and Kwan Yin invite us into a profound understanding of life, of coming into form and then leaving form. That process is inescapable. And the suffering implied is twinned with the compassion fundamental to the reality of the universe. Just look and listen, with an open heart.

A note on voices here. When Manjushri suggested I receive a new set of Teachings on compassion, he said it would include Teachings from him, from Kwan Yin, and from me.

At first I was startled by this new form, but soon I realized how well it would reflect my many conversations with each of them.

Noah's Wife

Yes, we can begin now. We have many things we would like to teach you. Today we will start with a Teaching about the relationship between compassion and suffering, or, as you have named it, the missing voice of the feminine. We will teach you about the source of compassion and its embeddedness in the feminine. And so, we must speak of male and female, the rule of the fathers, and the essential equilibrium between masculine and feminine that must be established.

Your world faces an intense crisis: the very survival of civilized human life as you know it is at risk. Many thinkers are deeply aware of this and argue passionately on behalf of environmental consciousness and the needs of the poor and the marginal, alarmed by the deep gulfs opening between those with much and those with little. Time and space have become claustrophobic, as more and more recognize the limits pressing in on them. Some respond in horror and fear; some respond with denial and escape; and some respond with violence and greed. Never has it been more important for people to stand still, open their minds and hearts to the fullest consciousness possible, and then to begin to create a world based on reality. Never before has humanity faced such a decision point. You must remember it is not necessary for everyone to come to this awareness, only that there be enough of you, aware and conscious, to be able to shift the balance of the world mind and energies. One fully conscious person has much more impact on the world around her, energetically, than she can possibly imagine, whereas the unconscious person has little. After all, that is one meaning of "unconscious," to be disconnected from the world systems of mind and energy.

You have in your religious tradition the old story of the Great Flood, when God wearied of people and decided to clear out the planet and start over with "his" project. The planetary crisis you face today is perhaps of similar mythic scope, but this is not a time for Noah or his solution. Noah invited only his own family to join him on his ark. It is precisely that kind of thinking which has led to your current crisis: save the near and dear, and the rest be damned! Noah may have saved a tiny portion of creation with his gesture, but it was a gesture of ego, of little mind. His guilt for surviving the devastation has permeated the karmic inheritance of all his descendants, and he remains an image of ego-limited solutions to planetary problems.

The human task ever since, as every religious tradition testifies, has been to break open that tightly constricted heart and mind until the fullness of life can flow in. This has been the deep theme of human history, the work of the world's teachers and holy ones, and the spirited quest of the world's seekers. Every powerful story about the human condition probes this issue. Noah reveals the emergence of ego and male domination, and ever since humans have wrestled with how to civilize ego, in all its dimensions.

Please note: ego is not to be destroyed, for it is also the vehicle of new consciousness. Noah heard the voice: "Prepare for the flood," and he responded as instructed. The journey of consciousness cannot and must not go backwards. One may yearn for Eden or Shambhala, but one must not struggle to return there. The way leads out and forward, towards ever more consciousness; not backward to immersion again in species life. Few wish to take up that task, for the way towards more consciousness is arduous and often painful. But let us say again: enough of you are now walking that path, that subtle and significant energy shifts are well under way.

So why would we suggest a Teaching on the hidden Divine Feminine? What we have said so far is a brief restatement of the main point of your first long Teaching from us. The problems facing humans were sketched there with a very broad stroke. The students must understand the larger context of their worries about their world. What is needed now is a deeper discussion of the medicine, if you will, for these problems. In the first volume, we taught about the current situation. Here, we will discuss some of the deep origins of these world-threatening problems and then tell a story that might help you to re-imagine ways to move forward and to open to the Heart Center. If the first volume was the Wisdom Teachings, then this one will be the Compassion Teachings. Wisdom and compassion must balance and join. Ignorance must be dissipated and the heart center must fling open all its windows and doors. This Teaching is the next step of this project.

What might we see between the lines of Noah's story? Noah's wife did not want to get on the ark. She argued long and hard for other ways, especially, to argue with God. But her main point was that she and Noah must remain with their people and, as a community, create another response. Stubborn Noah refused, insisting it would be better to save themselves than for all to perish in the promised flood. That is masculine thinking—focused, intentional, responsible for those dependent upon him, and pragmatic. Very pragmatic. Noah's wife (and note that we do not even know her name) is silenced, and her voice does not appear in the text. How could she have been silent? She faced leaving behind her friends, her rich network of community, her gardens and the neighborhood children, bird song and the elders she visited. How could she be silent? But Noah did not listen and could not listen, or he would have been unable to build his great ark and gather in the species he would protect. Many creatures pleaded with him for a berth. Except for a pair of each kind, he refused them all.

We wish now to retrieve the voice of Noah's wife: the compassionate one, with a different kind of courage in her willingness to face the wrathful Deity and argue for a change of course. She insisted they should remain embedded in their community and share in its suffering and danger. Hers is the fearless heart in the story, not Noah's frenzied construction of an ark to ride out the storm. Wall Street is not the answer. Technology is not the answer. Stealing the resources of others is not the answer. War is not the answer. Compassion is rooted in the experience of one's own suffering. Pity is the response to others' suffering. Only when you realize that there is no separation between self and other—that another's suffering is also your own—only then can there be compassion. Boarding the ark is an act of separation. This time, there is no ark. This time, the only response possible is that of Noah's wife. That is what we call, the compassion of the Divine Feminine. And so we begin.

(It is an absolutely gorgeous morning; the Great Lake is calm and the air is sweet. I have dragged myself to the sofa and my laptop, to start receiving the new material. It is always so difficult at the start. The energy is challenging; there is so much else I would rather do—clear out some brush that blocks my view of the lake, weed a year's worth from the peonies, or go for a kayak ride. But I promised myself, I will sit down quietly and listen. It is hard, this combination of alert listening and holding my mind as calm, empty and undisturbed as I can. Otherwise my language interferes with reception. Language, always language. What separates us from other species, and what can so often separate us from each other.)

Noah's wife wished to stay with her community, and if necessary, suffer together. In its simplest meaning, compassion means to suffer with. That is the feminine way. The masculine way is to treat the sufferer as an object, "over there," and then to offer sympathy or pity. That distances the suffering, rather than bringing it close. There are moments when that is appropriate; one cannot always choose to suffer with. Limits reflect the emotional and psychological capacity of each person; each must learn her own limits and respect them. There is no blame in that. In fact, it reflects discernment and good judgment, both crucial aspects of wisdom.

There is one other preliminary issue. Humans have imaged the feminine aspect of the divine as a deity, a goddess. She is the receptive phase of how the fundamental energy of the cosmos circulates. She receives all energy and then sends it back out, in the great and infinite pulse of all that is. She is "before form." Because all forms return to her as well, humans have imagined her to be dark, as in opaque and impenetrable, the receptacle of forms, invisible and unknowable. Fear of formlessness is engraved in every living being. Humans know that death, decay, and dissolution are aspects of formlessness, and they learned to associate all that with the realm of the Goddess and her inscrutable dark face.

But that is just one portal into her realm. Humans only recognize this aspect of her, and because they fear death, they color her dark and fear her. Little mind or ego recognizes its own impermanence and the brevity of an embodied life, and fills with terror. Some of that terror is projected out onto the Goddess, and she becomes the Dark Goddess: Kali, the witch, the dangerous shaman, Erishkagal with her eyes of death, and many others.

Let us stop and clarify. To begin with "there is form and there is formlessness," though even that is not the true beginning. The true beginning is that there is only One, and it manifests into forms out of its formlessness. None of this is substantial, however; for each continually transforms into the other. All is process, and all that is moves constantly into and out of form. At any particular moment, form is shifting towards formlessness, and formlessness has already begun to give birth to form. This great pulse, which is the cosmos, has long been a foundational insight of Eastern wisdom. Now very advanced Western scientists probing the fundamental nature of matter search for scientific language to describe what they too now can see, if not fully understand: that matter exists only instant by instant. It is the potentiality of a bit of energy to dissolve and then to form, to dissolve and then to form. At every level of matter, from deep within the heart of the atom to the very circulation of galaxies, there is only this pulse.

Ancients around the world intuited some aspect of this pulse and named its two poles male and female. That reflected the nature of their bodily experience; it was a naming system right at hand. And it pointed to the mystery of opposites joining to create a new being. How better to express complex energetic transformations?

But it was a poetic or metaphoric naming, at least initially. Male and female is analogous with a dimly grasped insight into the fundamental nature of reality. But nothing is as ephemeral as the instruction to remember that it is only a metaphor. The male/female dichotomy hardened conceptually in two ways: what was first grasped as continual movement, indeed, as a pulse, solidified into opposite poles, firm and eternal. And what was named via a simplified sexual system became the oldest system of projection and re-identification. The projections too solidified into firm "realities" of male and female governing the universe, then deities requiring propitiation and eventually increasingly rigid social structures and habits of mind.

Now humans find themselves living within a set of enclosed conceptual structures, each one contained within another, and then another, all reflecting the fundamental insight of the dance between form and formlessness, but named with ever with more fierceness as the eternal dichotomies of male and female. The repercussions were legion. On one hand, it threw up virtually insurmountable obstacles to grasping the nature of reality. On the other, it forced most of human life into a gendered structure: tasks, behaviors, moral codes, and the division of labor, on one hand, all the way to basic consciousness and self-knowledge, on the other.

The division of the primordial One into two allowed for the explosion of human knowledge and human consciousness. How did that come to be named male and female, and how did that, in turn, shape human life and even consciousness? Such human perceptions penetrated every aspect of human society, and at any historical moment, the gendered naming of reality facilitated some aspects of consciousness and inhibited others. The historical process has been what it has been. But the moment has arrived, in your lifetime, for thoughtful observers to peel back that first and oldest projection and to try to understand how completely it has shaped human experience.

Many others work on this project; scholars and activists, daughters and wives struggle to name what is not "natural" but "conventional" about the profound gendering of human life, and when properly named, to begin to dissolve it where it obstructs the expansion of consciousness. Our project now, with your cooperation, will be a contribution to that larger process of de-gendering and re-naming much human behavior and mental life.

Essentially, there will be two parts to this project: first, we will probe the projections on and the names of the great container of form/formlessness, the unformed Divine Feminine. We will examine her dark aspects, as humans experience her. We hope to peel back some of the human fears about formlessness, in order to catch a glimpse of the profound receptivity and creativity that lie behind it. She receives all that is, while giving birth to all that is; She allows all that has potential form to emerge into form (to use a non-gendered set of phrases). Nothing is to be rejected or discarded. All is process, and all constantly transforms. There is no stasis; there is nothing permanent except the processes of transformation from form to formlessness and back again to form. The Goddess, despite your prayers, does not protect you from this, but welcomes it; indeed, she **is** it. People pray to her for protection from the constant change, but it cannot be controlled or interrupted Her answer to that prayer is to teach you all to see more clearly. That includes your Teachers.

Beings resist learning this. Why? Because beings in form prefer form to formlessness. What is gained from a stable center of consciousness and the accumulation of insight is infinitely precious. But your appreciation of stability generates attachment to being in form, and then, the dance gets tricky. Those who can must learn more intricate steps, balancing lightly between the two views. They earn the name "adepts." Their mind and being are playful, for they know the truth of the Dark Goddess and how she embraces change and impermanence.

The other part of this Teaching will be a more pointed analysis of the heavy weight of the gendered system on human life. Some of this you already know. What you know analytically must be brought home, so we will discuss the burdens of patriarchy and the gendered world in your own life and self-understanding. Some of this you will recognize, and some will be new to you.

Then last, we will ask how all this has shaped humans' understanding of wisdom and compassion, the tasks and qualities traditionally distributed according to a gendered division of labor among both deities and earthly humans. This deserves some careful thinking, for it will turn out to be a powerful tool for shifting the fate of the human species and thus the well-being of the planet as a whole. We want to excavate compassion, where it has been buried along with the threatening feminine and return it to human society. We want to restore voice and agency to Noah's wife, in the lives and voices of countless students. Only that can push back the flood.

This is of necessity not a linear argument, but rather a nest of arguments, one within the next. Just as you struggled with *The Wisdom Teachings*, only relaxing when you realized each topic was another spoke heading into the empty center, so this text will also develop its own complex logic and form. Please be patient with us as we try to separate what is a single piece to us into discrete parts, so you can grasp it in all its complexity. Then, we will help you reassemble it into a single whole. Please remember the complex form that is emerging is part of what generates resistance in you; your mind literally cannot hold it in its entirety. Or better said: your mind actually does intuit and glimpse it in its wholeness, but is overwhelmed by the difficulty of translating it into language with its sentences in linear form.

I am wondering, what shall I call you? I can't name your energy or presence. It doesn't seem strange or overpowering, but I am tired after an hour of receiving your Teaching. May I ask, who are you?

Of course, you may ask. This is the Manjushri energy again. You don't recognize it because it has been a long time since we worked together. You find it less strenuous than it was for you several years ago. This is good, and we are glad. This project will go easily. And we remind you, there are more projects awaiting you, when you have time and energy. We also say to you, we are deeply grateful for your willingness to do this work with us. You help us bring very important messages into the human world. Though it may seem to you this is a very small piece, which is of little importance in the larger scheme, it is in truth a potent and fertile seed, which is sprouting everywhere it lands. It is worth continuing this work.

Let us begin with a story, one you have told when you spoke with prospective students and their families. You said, to help them understand the deep value of living and studying in a women's college, that it would help them identify the structures of the prevalent gender system. Just as a fish cannot describe water until it is removed from its life-long environment, so humans cannot describe how gender works until they are in the midst of a different version. The contrasts are jarring and often very instructive. Changing contexts, as you know, is one of the most powerful mechanisms for shifting people's consciousness.

You are aware of how gender roles and expectations shape styles of behavior and relationship. And you are alert to how gender systems constrict the choices of many of your international students, especially those from South Asia. You have thought long and hard about how gender worked in your family, and how it did and didn't pave the pathways of your life. You have followed the feminist critiques of traditional religious understandings and practices, seeking out those small cracks where women believers might recognize their own authority and dignity as spiritual seekers.

But there is much more for you to study and digest. We want to take you on a journey into the fundamental origins of gender and the gendering of mental processes. We want you to see how the original separation of male and female was applied first to mind and then to all derivative mental processes. This includes naming, categorization, concept-formation, and abstraction. It permeated the realms of the imagination, of narrative and dream, and of every impulse to touch the realms of the invisible, the unearthly, the Sacred.

Gender-free perception is not possible for humans. That said, we think we can open your eyes to deeper layers of your gendered world. This may seem a long way from a discussion of compassion, our announced theme for this extended Teaching. We will arrive there, even though we begin at the far end of this long thread. It will be like going backward, generation by generation, through a family tree, tracing the line of ancestors back to where the evidence is faint and illegible. When we arrive at our destination, the Dark Feminine, we will turn around and retrace our steps, but with clearer minds and restored hearts. All of humanity groans under the weight of gender and its multitude of consequences. To heal the world, to save the world from human exploitation and unconsciousness, we must restore the feminine. Humans must be able to envision wholeness. It is impossible now.

I just reread these first pages. I am astonished at their richness and complexity. What an astounding blessing and teaching.

Very good. For this must first be a helpful teaching for you. You are a highly engaged channel, not an unconscious one who simply takes down the message like a scribe and passes it on. Your ability to engage with these Teachings is a major reason why we chose you to receive them. As we have said before, you have prepared for this all your life, with your deep thoughtfulness and wide reading and teaching. The more you can inhabit your complex and intuitive mind, the more generative and satisfying your life.

You are carrying an image of an archeological excavation, the archeology of gender. It is a good one. You must begin on the surface, the most recently deposited layer, and examine it closely. Then, you can proceed downward, meticulously cataloguing the layers, understanding that you are also moving backwards in time to earlier and earlier remains. On the surface of contemporary society, you can see quite a bit of flux, as people negotiate shifts in their own personal relationships affected by gender. Men now take care of children, and women practice law and medicine. Men nurse dying patients, and women travel the world as leaders of whole countries. The rigid division of labor, labor as work, has softened considerably in your life time, so much so that there are those who say that the work of feminism has been accomplished. It takes only a few minutes of careful observation to see that is not true, but it is certainly true that some women (in the rich world, with ample access to education and training) have gained much more freedom to pursue their own life goals.

We see shifts in language, financial relationships and popular culture, for example, and struggles continue within the denser realms of religious practices and institutions, conceptions of leadership, and all that relates to human bodies, especially sexuality. There is no need to catalogue all these shifts in your society today, as every observer is well aware of them.

Instead, go down one more layer and brush off the surface material to glimpse what lies below. You will see that the fundamental structures of gender remain as robust as ever; what is changing is only the marginal content of male and female roles. A man "stays home" to care for his newborn; a woman becomes the oft-remarked CEO of a large corporation. Why are we interested? Because they are such startling exceptions to what is recognized as "normal." The norm is clearly defined; you still expect relatively firm boundaries between men's and women's work. That the boundaries are becoming slightly more permeable under the enormous pressure of reformers and legal requirements does not undermine the categories or the divisions of gender. It has released some pressure for change, while obscuring the tenacity of the categories.

There is another very significant factor: hierarchy, the relative power and value of the two categories. Noah didn't have to listen to his wife, and she had no choice but to join him on his ark. That is hierarchy, a power relationship as operative today as it was then. In a sentence, you might say, as long as the traditional gender hierarchy remains, small adjustments in the social definition of each gender role can be tolerated. If the dominant gender controls the actual division of labor and is able to reproduce its own dominance, there has been no real threat to nor any real change in the gender system. Only shifts in the hierarchical arrangements, especially in which gender gets to define gender roles, constitute significant change in the gender system.

There are now two salient dimensions to gender: the actual content of the separation of roles, activities, and responsibilities, on one hand, and the authority to shape and rank those categories, on the other. There is no extant society in the world today where men do not have the authority to maintain and rank the categories of gender. Certainly not all men, for other social categories split up the category of men, such as race, class, ethnic identity, religious practice, and political role. What we say here about how gender works is paralleled by those other systems of division and ranking. But gender is primary, and the rules and structures of gender are reproduced in other human arenas. In every case you might identify how the ruling group deploys its ability to define the categories and punish those who would rebel against the boundaries and their implicit or explicit hierarchical ranking. It is Noah's wife who is silenced, not Noah. And it is the Goddess who must go into the darkness, not the God. And as we shall see, what is silent, what is in the darkness, what cannot be seen, is what is feared. The cycle of control and repress, control and repress, has been launched, and human society begins to careen into ever more disequilibrium.

Probe down another layer. Take your soft bristle brush and remove the sediment of centuries. Here you find the dim outlines of mental concepts, of self-images, of myth, and sacred narratives. This layer teems with images of gender, if only they can be made visible to the human eye.

How can we pick our way through this great storehouse of human imagination and creativity? We are looking for a thread to follow, which will take us to the foundations, the original wellspring of gendered thinking. It began of course with human bodies, close at hand, but what led to turning those bodies into images of thought? It is an astounding conceptual move, indicative of the startling inventiveness of the emerging human mind. Why not plant and animal or day and night? Why not a triplet instead of a double, as the template for human concepts?

We see a fundamental duality built into the human organism. Consider how many organs are really dual: kidneys, eyes, ears, limbs, lungs, nostrils, adrenal glands, tonsils, and so many more. Perhaps it was originally a security system, with a back-up ready and close at hand, but eventually it would allow for a certain flexibility and complexity. But probably most important is the double hemispheres of the brain; even as layer after layer of neurological development continued, the brain seemed to "insist" on double hemispheres, with their parallel dependent neurologies. Humans think differently than other species, or perhaps a more accurate way to say that is that humans process information differently. All species have perfected particular kinds of sensation, of receiving and processing information. Some are sensitive to particular wave lengths; most have specialized visual or auditory abilities, and so on. Humans, unlike other species, receive particular information in one part of their brain, and then process it or categorize it with another part of the brain. Evaluation, discrimination, and judgment follow, integrating memory, learning and emotion. The complexity of these secondary processes distinguishes the human brain from that of other species.

It is also what distinguishes between human mental functioning and that of your Teachers, beings not in body. Because we do not exist in a three-dimensional world, we are free to receive simultaneously multiple streams of information, even independently of time and space. We have found it nearly impossible to describe this to our students, and since it is not germane to our task here, we will leave it. Suffice it to say, because the parameters of our perception are significantly different from those of humans, we are puzzled by the dichotomous, gendered structures of so much of human perception and conceptualization. We realize the extent to which so much of human mental processing goes through the filter of gender, but we do not understand why it continues to this day, even if it were once a significant evolutionary accomplishment or invention.

Modern thinkers of the last century or so have looked into the human past for some clues about this. Their theories each have a grain of truth: anxiety about reproduction and birth; power of human sexuality or sexual desire; acquaintance with death; and fear of the unknown, the dark, and the invisible. But they too stumble trying to reach beyond the written and visual record. Anthropologists and depth psychologists have been of some help, even as they recognize how intuitive their explanations are and how likely to be shaped by their own cultural assumptions.

Perhaps the second question is easier to answer: how did the dichotomy of gender become a hierarchy of gender, and what did that serve? There the simple answer seems correct: that men were bigger and stronger in important physical ways and they were able to translate that into primacy. Perhaps first, a man exercised power over an individual woman. Only later would it generalize so men as a group dominated women as a group. That shift is certainly lost in the murky first millennia of human life, though it would be extremely interesting to understand how that happened.

We can then imagine how the human capacities for imagination and narrative come into play, as earthly gender roles are projected upon non-earthly images. Invisible beings are identified and named; local spirits, gods and goddesses, and their denizens in the "other world" tended fertility and protected the group from harm. Those very deities would come to rule human life, explaining the community's origins, legitimating human practices and requiring propitiation, devotion, and obedience. It is no surprise that those human values projected on the invisible beings would return to earth, like rain, reinforcing those very values as if delivered from on high. This constantly self-reinforcing process created the firmest structure in human cognition, apart from self/other (though it too came to be shaped and colored by gender). The ubiquitous experience of gender (and we really mean sexual differentiation here) reinforced the sense that dichotomies are natural and function in the real world in some fundamental and substantial way. Likewise it seemed apparent that most dichotomies include a hierarchical ranking, such that one part of the dyad is superior to the other.

By now, this pattern has been reinforced for thousands and thousands of years, replicated in language, in all human relationships, in social structures and emerging institutions, in the distribution of power and authority, and in the very constitution of communities and community self-understandings. And because what is below reflects what is above, and vice versa, the deities play out the same roles, the same divisions of labor, and articulate the same values and meanings as are found in the earthly communities. It provided a stable equilibrium, a container within which great experimentation and inventiveness were possible in the realms of agriculture, language, arts, technology, warfare, and ritual. Gender and its implicit privileging of the male became the essential marker of human thought and behavior; it is no surprise it similarly permeated the realms of the gods.

The Human Mind: Analysis and Synthesis

We have seen how gender provides a system of naming and interpretation and for understanding many aspects of human life. The next question, a much more difficult one, is whether gender distinctions actually exist in human bodies, in human beings beyond the behaviors taught through socialization? This raises some complicated issues.

Let's start by saying, there are both masculine and feminine ways for mind to function. Because both women and men can use both kinds of mental functioning, we must use "masculine," not "male," and ""feminine," not "female."

The .masculine mind separates and names. Many cognitive processes—such as discrimination, conceptualization, categorization, and fundamentally, analysis—illustrate this. You remember that analysis means simply taking a complex item apart into its constituent pieces. This allows complexity to be broken down into less complex parts, thus opening the way to investigation. The scientific method is the jewel of these mental processes, with its careful rules for purposeful investigation and experimentation. Most humans walk; some run; some run well, becoming skillful athletes; and some can run a marathon. Similarly, all humans can think; some can work with categories and concepts; some can create new concepts and categories; and some—the marathon runners—practice science.

May we remind you that science is only one way to understand reality. Its power and success derive from its disciplined method of investigation. It insists on excluding all forms of subjectivity, for example, and with that absolute rule of evidence, it also excludes much that is learned through feminine mental functioning. An important purpose of our Teaching is to legitimate other ways to investigate an expanded understanding of reality.

The first tool the masculine mind picks up is dichotomy. And its first knowledge of dichotomy is gender. Old Noah invited pairs of animals on to the ark, each pair a male and female. That is where this ancient myth begins, unless one wishes to repair to the Garden of Eden. From the original unity emerges differentiation. Though the Creation story says, "Male and female He created them," the first two, Adam and Eve, don't seem to notice for some time. You might read that myth to mean, human life is meant to traverse the long road back to a recognition of that primal unity, otherwise named, the path of human consciousness. All the rest is side trips and sub plots.

Feminine mental functioning differs from masculine mental functioning. Please remember, we are referring to a quality of mind, not how any particular man or woman actually thinks. These are "models" or "ideal types." We could just as accurately name it X thinking and Y thinking, but you would find, empirically, that X was largely distributed among those of one sex and Y in those of the other. This is not yet fully understood, and contemporary evolutionary biologists, neuroscientists, feminist sociologists and behavioral psychologists are all probing this puzzle. It seems increasingly clear that sexual and gender differentiation are both complex continua, and not dichotomous categories as many have long assumed.

Our purpose here is to discuss the implications of those two kinds of thinking, especially how the dominance of one has shaped modern human life. Then we will suggest ways to recover access to the subordinated style of mental functioning; only that can begin to heal the human psyche and human societies. If retrieving the banished feminine is possible, as we believe it is, it should also be possible for humans to create a much more sustainable relationship with the Earth. We are looking far into the future, and we wish to facilitate your ability to do the same. This will give you courage and hope, essential to do the hard work of creating a saner world.

And why do we, beings outside of time and space, care about all of this? The simple answer is consciousness. We too long for humans to wake up and to recognize their interdependence with all living beings. As pure consciousness ourselves, it is our nature to include humans and all sentient beings within our field of awareness. We prompt our students to become more conscious, and to see that each and all are enfolded in the great unity of the cosmos.

Feminine mental functioning differs from masculine mental functioning in several ways. First, it does not divide. It does not impose a dichotomy upon every factor, experience, object, or feeling. It does not automatically judge every object of perception, naming it good or bad. Feminine mental life recognizes gestalts, entire settings or situations, grasping (though not necessarily naming) parts in their complex interrelationships and within the web of their connections. This mind does not separate first, and then conceptualize, categorize, evaluate or analyze. Rather, this mind perceives first a totality, a whole situation, catching even its feeling tones and underlying disturbances. This is an intuitive capability, responsive to energies and seeing deeply into or beyond what is immediately visible. We aren't referring to those highly developed and very special skilled seers, who can see at great distances or see a person's etheric body. We are describing a natural vision available to all human beings, but which is found more often among women. It requires no special training or giftedness, unless one's masculine, analytic thinking has become dominant. Then it might take some practice to develop its complement.

The Feminine and the Heart Center

What are the connections between feminine mental functioning and the heart center? Please remember that every culture locates thinking and feeling in particular places in the body, and there is little agreement about that. Some locate thinking in the head, and some in the chest, and some in the abdomen. Some locate the soul or the non-perishable part of a human being in the gut or the heart. Some insist soul is not contained with the body at all, but floats outside it, maintaining a connection, which dissolves at death.

What we see is that masculine mental functioning arises in a precise part of the human brain. In evolutionary terms, it is the most recent to emerge. It accounts for the staggering human accomplishments in agriculture, science, and technology. That part of the brain continues to develop neurologically. Vast amounts of learning are possible now, in a single lifetime. This highly specialized cognitive functioning differentiates humans from other species, including other primates. For some, it justifies human control of all planetary resources. One might name it "human exceptionalism," which can be deployed to justify patriarchal culture and practices.

Feminine mental functioning is also located in the brain, but it arises from complex neural communication networks, which link multiple centers of perception and interpretation. This is the neurological base for more integrated mental processing. Neuroscientists now understand that the hemispheres of the female brain have significantly more connective links than the male brain, whose hemispheres are more autonomous and independent of each other.

It is an error to think that feelings are heart-based. Not so. Feelings too are interpretations of more primary experiences in both the male and female brain. Nevertheless, there is also a significant relationship between the brain and heart center that is a necessary (though not sufficient) condition for well-developed feminine mental functioning.

The heart center must be open to what is before it, what is in its presence. It is a highly sensitive organ, which opens and closes at the slightest stimulus. In that, it resembles a light-sensitive flower or a sea anemone. The most accurate feminine perception is only possible when the heart center is open. If it is not, a critical range of information may be shut out, and the feminine mind can't function fully. Crucial areas of the brain, wired together to make possible feminine mental functioning, receive no "data" if the heart center is closed or shut down. The resulting gestalt then is incomplete, superficial, or clouded over with other extraneous material. It is actually that kind of feminine thinking that is mocked and dismissed in your society.

Some of you are aware of these problems. You work with projection, stereotype, prejudice, and other habits of mind as the result of a shut down or partially closed heart center. Removing these blockages is a core spiritual and psychological practice around the world. It is an urgent task today.

Let's probe this a little more deeply. If the feminine mind specializes in perceiving connections, then anything that reduces the horizons of perception, blocks information, or shuts out complexity will undermine those perceptions. Masculine mind requires the meticulous practice of rigorous analytic procedures to achieve its best knowledge. Feminine mind requires not only both hemispheres of the brain to be well connected and communicating, but also that brain and heart center also be well connected and communicating. To accomplish this at a high level is difficult, not only for men, but also for women. And if you add to that the fact that most of you live in societies that do not value this kind of mental functioning, it is easy to understand why there is so little feminine mental functioning in your culture and public discourse.

On the Nature of the Heart Center

Before we continue the Teaching on the two kinds of mental functioning, we must say a little about the heart center, for access to the heart center is jeopardized by an overwhelming reliance on masculine thinking. Feminine mental functioning, which requires close coordination with a lively heart center, is crucial for all we have been speaking of: healing, reducing suffering, awakening to interdependence, and creating a new, more vibrant culture.

The heart center is not a physical organ, in the usual sense. It cannot be harmed by a heart attack, for example, nor does it weaken with injury or old age. It is an energetic center, which receives, processes, interprets, and sends energy. It is a highly sensitive communications center; its capacities can be extended and refined through certain practices. It can also be dulled and even shrouded by certain life choices or karmic issues. We need not discuss those here.

We recognize athletes by their strong physical bodies, which they train daily over many years. They practice their sport and build their physique. Similarly, we can recognize a bodhisattva by her exquisitely developed heart center, her sensitivity to others' suffering and needs, and her skill at responding to those needs. There are many practices in the traditions of Tibetan Buddhism whose purpose is to "bulk up" the heart center and increase its sensitivity and responsiveness.

Every human is born with a functioning heart center, though in young children it is mostly a receptive organ. It is possible, though infrequent, to completely shut it down, through a poorly lived life. Even SS guards at the concentration camps were known to respond to classical music and to lovingly tend their families.

One might ask, what goes awry to cause someone's heart center to atrophy? Most often it begins with poor treatment as a child. Her needs and fears are not acknowledged by a sympathetic adult, and she learns she must push all that down, below the level of awareness, if she is to manage. Learning how to ignore, repress, or deny those difficult feelings creates a deep split between her natural experience of her life and her emerging understanding of what is necessary to enhance her stability and survival. Every human learns to do this in some degree, through social processes commonly named socialization and maturation. But too much denial and self-repression prevents the young person from exercising compassion towards herself and her difficulties. Without the foundation of self-compassion, it is unlikely that a person will be able to offer compassion to another.

Self-repression and self-criticism block the development of compassion because they starve the heart center. On the other hand, without some emotional and psychological maturity, a person finds it difficult to find the right balance between her own needs and the needs of others. The spiritual path in most religious traditions is centrally focused on this issue: how to encourage compassion for others, which requires a certain level of self-care, while reinforcing the fundamental understanding that in the end, there is no conflict between self and other.

How does this connect with the heart center? The heart center is the organ of compassion, the complex organ that perceives suffering in both self and other and chooses to respond. To function in an optimal way it must be closely linked to the human brain, for the brain's perceptual skills are essential. The decision to act to relieve someone's suffering requires mental functioning joined to the sensitive perceptiveness of the heart center.

To say it differently: if a person cannot experience her own suffering, and then respond kindly to herself, she will eventually build up such a callous on her heart center or such a thick wall of denial, she will lose her ability to sense another person's suffering or to realize its severity. She will then be unable to respond effectively to the other person's suffering. Unable to respond compassionately, her life becomes ever more constricted, superficial, and unsatisfying.

What is the medicine for this? She must learn to recognize and experience her own suffering, in order to recognize and respond to the suffering of others. She must exercise her own heart center, day after day, to build up its scope and strength and to increase its connections with the brain's mental functioning.

Two Kinds of Mental Functioning

We can return now to our discussion of the two kinds of mental functioning, and their implications for the culture and society in which you live. The masculine mind works out of highly specialized centers in the brain, which allows it to focus, analyze, differentiate, and investigate. This is where reason and logic are most centrally housed. The feminine mind, on the other hand, not only uses the web of connections between the two hemispheres of the brain, but it also requires strong connectivity with the heart center and its different kind of perception. These two kinds of mental functioning (and we must remind you and our readers that a person can develop both kinds) are very different in the breadth and depth and quality of their perception. It is similar to how different visual systems are sensitive to different parts of the spectrum of light.

These two forms of perception support different kinds of awareness. One is highly focused on the visible world, and the other gathers in less specific information about a wider and less materially defined reality. All humans, both women and men, can develop and use both kinds of perception and awareness.

Throughout human history there have been exceptionally gifted individuals who have accomplished this, despite the limitations of their own society and culture. And in most pre-modern societies there was room for them to develop their gifts, as a shaman, healer, or prophet. The boundaries between the two kinds of mental functioning were more porous. Nor were they usually rigidly gendered. But with the great explosion of scientific thinking in the early modern period, several things shifted which brought you to the state you are in now.

Analytic thinking made an enormous leap with the emergence of science. The twin projects of mathematics and physical science fed each other's gathering analytic power and discoveries, both useful and deeply intriguing. Because it required years of education and further training to participate in scientific inquiry, and because formal education was only available to boys, the gendering of scientific thinking was unavoidable.

Those without access to that kind of education were left to develop their own forms of perception and insight. Some worked with their society's traditional knowledge; some could develop new subtle forms of perception; and some pursued their own ways of exploring the vast horizon of their reality. But their mental functioning retained its rootedness in the sensitive heart center. It was synthetic and inclusive (where masculine thinking is analytic and discriminating) and feeling-toned and value-sensitive (where masculine thinking prides itself on its rigorous search for objectivity). This is what we are calling feminine mental functioning, the view of Noah's wife.

Let us remind you again: that there are two forms of mental functioning is helpful and not problematic. What is problematic is that one form now dominates your social, political, and economic world, and the other has been silenced and rejected. The analytic thinking which fuels science, materialist thinking and economic development (and capitalism), torn loose from its partnership with the inclusive, gestalt perceptiveness arising from feminine awareness, has become extremely destructive to human well-being and the life of the planet. That is the problem.

It is unfortunately easy, when facing a system dramatically pulled to an extreme, to overcorrect. Early feminists, who decried male dominance and celebrated what they imagined to be a primal female consciousness, did not really offer a viable solution. Their critique, however, was enormously valuable. Their project, truly revolutionary, is one of the most complex humans have ever faced. Power asymmetries, gender roles, reproduction and sexuality, inequities distributed by class and race, and cultural and linguistic practices—to name just a few—are tightly woven into the very fabric of modern civilization. We welcome what they have begun, and we support all of you who struggle to restore the balance between masculine and feminine and male and female. It is an essential part of the healing necessary now to avert the approaching catastrophe for human and planetary survival.

A Brief Summary

Let us briefly retrace the steps of our argument: We began by noting the marked differences between two kinds of mental functioning, generally identified with male and female, the analytic and the synthetic or holistic. We noted how that became assigned to gender roles, probably very early in human history via the projected narratives about gods and goddesses. In the early modern period, with the explosion of scientific inquiry, the categories became much more rigid. Analytic or scientific knowledge acquired ever more social, economic and political power, deepening the divisions between the sexes in the gender system, as well as the divisions between the two kinds of mental functioning. What should have been joined together in a roughly balanced, complementary system was broken apart, with one kind assuming superiority and dominating the other. It is the long-term consequences of the hardening distinctions and then the domination of one by the other, which has drawn our attention and stimulated this long teaching.

Patriarchy and the Dominance of Masculine Thinking

We have here a very powerful, self-reinforcing feedback system of these forms of mental functioning and the related emergent social and political practices, which become the institutions of patriarchy. We must uncover its many layers, so we can focus on the centrality of compassion for human well-being and sustainable environments.

Let's circle through the preliminaries one more time. One of the great strengths of masculine thinking is that its preference for logic, clarity, and precision pushes us to separate out complex processes into smaller concepts and causal mechanisms. These must be laid out in linear sequences, so we can discuss them one at a time. Even syntax is pushed and shoved to wrestle these very slippery ideas into some conceptual and grammatical form that can be communicated clearly. You must receive our non-linear forms of communication and translate them into words and sentences. It is no wonder you find this strenuous.

So, how did these dimensions of patriarchy emerge? First, both women and men are born with innate personal preferences for certain kinds of thinking. Then, those preferences are shaped and filtered through the gender system. Gendered practices of thought become more visible and reinforce social and political practices. Eventually a stable system of gender and identity emerges. By then, one version has become dominant, and the system privileges what is male and masculine. And last, cultural forms—most significantly, religious and cultural systems—emerge to legitimate these structures of dominance. So the circle is complete.

Why did this become so problematic? There are two ways to look at this: what it did, and what it inhibited. The latter has caused more damage, as the disequilibrium expanded exponentially. Any possibility of complementarity vanished. And the cost of disempowering and silencing one half the population is of course immeasurable. When you consider that this has also marginalized all that rises from the heart center, one can barely imagine the cost of such radical inequality.

But the puzzle remains: how did certain kinds of thinking impact social and economic development? There seems to have been a link between the emergence of male dominance and the profound shift from the nomadic life of hunter/gatherers and more permanent agriculture. This allowed for more complex divisions of labor and eventually the possibility of surplus, which sowed the seeds of a more complex human society. It may also have been the moment that the gender hierarchy and structured inequality emerge. Those privileges would require legitimacy backed by the use of force. By the time we meet Noah, there are domesticated animals, husbands and wives, and agriculture. Nomads and hunters/gatherers would have sensed the rising water and left the area. Farmers couldn't.

In the patriarchal world, human society is modeled on and governed by the dominant religious narrative. We see there the centrality of the male gods with their powers of creation (usurped, of course, from the great earth goddesses before them), law- giving and judgment. As defenders of the community, they preside over conflicts and war. They are fierce about boundaries, distinguishing between insiders and foreigners, between rulers and ruled, between the good and the bad, and between men and women.

Their supporting narratives began as a small seed, a slight fantasy, perhaps, in the mind of a powerful leader in some distant historical moment. But it developed in complexity and reach, as we have discussed earlier, until it displaced all other myths within the community culture and claimed interpretive primacy. By that, we mean, it claimed the right to interpret all other stories, myths, and practices. With that claim, it had finally established itself as the reigning cultural and religious practice.

Because this religious system legitimated the rule of individual men, both in the community and in the smaller groups organized around reproduction and early forms of property, such as the family and kinship groups, it also cleared the way for the mental functioning most common to men also to dominate. This too we have already discussed. So, the layers of domination stacked up, with huge implications for women. It defined women's status in the family and in the community; it elevated men and masculine functioning in every setting. Only men had access to the sacred, its precincts, texts, and practices. Men controlled sexuality and determined what could be included in elite culture. The sons of Adam continued to claim the right to name things, from their children to their own significance.

In all things, men and the masculine dominated women and the feminine. But domination does not mean extinction. The feminine was not obliterated, only pushed into dark corners of human consciousness. Masculine mental functioning dominated, at least in the public realms of authority, power, and distribution of resources. Feminine mental functioning, though certainly available to men, was usually limited to women, to be exercised in their more private spaces. The separation of the sexes, common in developed patriarchal societies, intensified these divisions, but it did allow for women's social and cultural spaces. There the affairs of the heart center could be cultivated, including the crucial care of children and the elderly. Stories of compassion and generosity to others were passed on to succeeding generations. None of this was hidden from men or disallowed by them, but it was of little significance to them.

There are many societies where women's rich but marginal traditions have survived.

All this you and your readers know. Unearthing this story has been a major accomplishment of contemporary feminist scholarship. It is extremely valuable, and must be taught widely. Understanding this long history can nourish and inspire profound changes to contemporary gender practices.

Such radical change, indeed revolutionary change, must begin with individuals. First comes a shocking recognition of one's own bias and how deeply patriarchal values have been planted everywhere one looks. Even that is a significant accomplishment, like a fish recognizing water. One powerful way to see this is to really recognize the limits of human freedom, the lopsidedness of public life, and the steady destruction of the Earth. There is the evidence of the overwhelming consequences of having relegated the feminine to the dark edges of human society. With the narrow tools of analytic masculine thinking, humans have built an unlivable world. There is scant room for the insight and depth of the heart center so characteristic of feminine perception and awareness.

The excavation has surely begun, but there is enormous work to be done in a very short time, if the Earth is to be healed and human communities are to be reconstituted. One might say that the Dark Goddess and the Divine Feminine, long exiled since the patriarchy first stretched its limbs and organized its world, is stirring in her underground domain. Perhaps the whole planet will find its new equilibrium, heedless of the implications for human life if it must be so. Perhaps the human psyche is breaking under the inhuman pressures of this high-tech, relentless economy and society. Many people have been aroused in the night by the cries of the suffering, human and non-human. The story clothing this awakening, this shift in awareness, must fit each listener; there will be many more. But each must begin by activating the heart center, one person at a time.

Activating the Heart Center

We welcome your continued opening and deepening, which facilitates our work and our partnership. The more receptive you are and the more of you available for this work, the easier and the more profound and powerful it can be. It all, of course, rests on the energetic capacities available, both to receive and to transmit and translate and send on. Your receptive capacities are expanding rapidly, and this allows us to engage with you in more ways and on more levels. Though you have experienced a great deal in these last several years, you have still barely put your foot in the water of what is available. We hope some day you will find yourself swimming!

We turn now to the central theme of this project: the heart center as an organ of perception and interpretation and its relationship to the practices of compassion. The underlying thread, to which we will return again and again, is suffering, the suffering of humans, all sentient beings, and the planet, which holds you all.

First, an anatomy lesson: where is the heart center in this system of energies we call a human being? You must realize you are a system of interlocking "bodies," each centered on a particular range of energy frequencies. Only one—the physical body—can be sensed through your five senses.

The next higher set of energy frequencies composes the emotional body. It is not normally visible to human sight, though some people are able to see its outlines. Next is the mental body, which is, again, composed of higher frequencies. Inter-penetrating all of these is the etheric body, with its high-frequency energies vibrating rapidly.

There are more, but we wish to focus on the heart center. These subtle bodies both surround each other, like those familiar Russian dolls, and inter-penetrate each other. They interact with each other as electrical pulses and waves do. This is difficult for your three-dimensional mind to visualize. Imagine it as a complicated string quartet, weaving melodic lines in and out, each distinct, yet also in profound and powerful relationship with each other, creating a complex whole. The heart center is one of two very powerful points of connection among these subtle bodies; the other is a point just above the head, where energies can also freely flow back and forth among the subtle bodies.

The usual state of affairs for most people is great congestion around the heart center; it may even be so heavily layered with obstructions that it can barely function. Moments of resonance with other energy bodies may be quite rare. Yet when those obstructions are cleared away, a connection with the higher bodies is revealed. Removing the obstructions allows for deep healing and makes possible new insight, epiphanies and sensitivities. It is a way to describe awakening; for the heart center is the royal road of awakening, which leads to what the ancients have named enlightenment.

And as you proceed along that royal road of healing towards the cosmic Heart Center, you become more skillful and highly tuned to higher frequencies of energy. Gradually identification with the physical body lessens, and you will gain more access to your emotional and mental life. That in turn offers more opportunity for deep healing, a more complex understanding of past lives, and the threads of relationship wound through them. There is much to encounter, recognize, evaluate, amend and then release. It is long and arduous work.

That work has its deep rewards, for the student is also gaining ever more stable access to a very wide view of reality. She now will become familiar with its fundamental qualities of compassion, wisdom and interconnectedness.

The heart center within, then, reveals a path, an artery of connection, and a circulatory system among the subtle energy bodies. It is also a first map of new consciousness.

This does not apply only to human beings. All beings share some aspects of multi-layered being. You are not just imagining certain forms of communication with your dog. You are not just imagining that the trees form a circle of protection around you when you are taking great risks of spirit. You are not just imagining that you can heave your deepest laments out into the Great Lake, and know relief and calm afterwards. Your subtle bodies are in harmonic resonance with similar energetic patterns in animals, plants and the Earth. Why would that not be the case?

That is a serious question. Why does your culture hold so fast to the opposite assumption, that there is no possibility of communication with other life forms? Is there any more arrogant form of ego imaginable?

In sum, then: opening the heart center within and following its lead into higher frequencies of energy is the path of awakening. It provides access to the most highly refined truth about Reality. And walking that path is also walking into deeper and deeper healing of body, emotions, mind and spirit.

Teachings from Kwan Yin and Penny Gill

The Springs of Compassion

Penny begins: This is a hinge moment in my active life, as I put down my first career and wait for the outlines of the next phase of my life to become clear. So it is a good moment to also gather up the core of my thinking about my world and its troubled times.

The central underlying problem of our culture, indeed, perhaps of Western civilization, is the increasingly great price we are paying for having so thoroughly rejected and repressed an entire realm of human experience. Though as short-hand I will name it the "dark feminine," that may well cause more analytic problems than it solves, and it may need a new name. But I believe our culture and thought are deeply gendered, and we can see the patterns of male dominance in public life, in the hegemonic role of science, and the insistence that what can be seen and counted takes precedence over the immaterial and the non-quantifiable.

My country, the richest the world has ever known, is riven by endemic violence, poor health, extremes of inequality, raging psychiatric disorders, and widespread discontent and fearfulness. Many of us are defeated by markets and market decisions. We are told, greed, inequality, exploitation, and widespread anxiety are normal consequences of living with freedom.

But we are not free, and we do not thrive. We are no longer admired or even respected in the world. We force on others what we do not practice ourselves. Our arrogance abroad no longer reflects our domestic accomplishments or way of life. Many Americans recognize we have lost our way, and that there is some fundamental error in our ways. And many Americans urge each his or her own solution to this.

As do I.

I believe our society, and now I must toss my cloak over what we blithely name the West and the post-modern world, is perilously one-sided and off-balance. It operates according to a canon of competition, invention, individualism, consumption, and domination. It draws its sustenance and values from scientific modernity and corporate and market freedom. It starves the life of the mind and denigrates the life of the heart. We destroy ourselves from the inside out.

We must, of course, heal ourselves before we can heal our world. What might that require? I believe, it requires finding again our heart centers, peeling away the layers of fear and distrust, and allowing that rich sensory and deliberative organ to add its perceptiveness, insight, and authority to our conscious lives. This is an easy sentence to write, but the effort involved to do that is significant. It takes great courage, perseverance, and a certain ease and comfort with the radical. It can frighten your friends and arm your enemies. But there is no other way. Either we break open our hearts to discover the fountains of compassion and kindness within, or we literally destroy ourselves and our world. Either we retrace our steps back to our origins, excavating our original "double face" of masculine and feminine, or we die stranded in our materialist desert.

I come to you, beloved Teacher, because I believe you speak from within that great stream of radical understanding and fierce compassion. You are both patient and ruthless. You do not tolerate untruth or self-deception. You are unmoved by our desire for security and control, and difficulty does not interest you. You have led me out of my very safe life that I might become truly radical, an outlaw, exhilarated by the winds of freedom.

I come to you because I think you will give me the words I can bring to my world, the words that might shed a different light on all that has seemed ordained and natural, words that might encourage more of us to revision our world. We must give voice to what has been silenced and give homage to what has been denigrated. We must restore some balance to our inhospitable lives, that we can create a world where everyone can be at home.

I do not know if you are a goddess, a manifestation of a timeless archetype, or a visitation from some parallel universe. I do know that your insights and guidance have been life-giving to me for many years. Now I must bring your voice out into the world for any who might find there energy and affirmation. I would ask of you, then, that you give me Teachings that I might share with others, about the Divine Feminine, the Heart Center, and all that is missing from our humanity in this rapidly globalizing world.

She laughs, long and warmly. Yes, indeed, you have thought deeply about these issues for a very long time. It is certainly time to bring them forward, and I am happy to help. Perhaps you now see how very much you "did" during your recent sabbatical, which you oddly insist on describing as without any "work." When, before now, might you have written these pages?

And Kwan Yin continues her response.

Form and Formlessness

Compassion is what holds the visible world in place. Compassion welcomes the emergence of forms. Without compassion, the core vibration of reality, there would be nothing. But what comes into form also must leave form, and that causes suffering. So the constant breath of being, into form and out of form, is actually the rhythm and breath of compassion and suffering. Neither can be known in isolation from the other. Any one who would turn away from suffering, in that moment, also rejects the possibility of compassion.

The masculine way is to detach from forms in order to study and understand them. This is cognition and the basis of analysis and science. Much deeper is the feminine way, which enters form fully in order to grasp the breath of the universe and the emergence and dissolution of forms. There are many entrances to this deep inquiry: contemplating the mind in meditation is one, and watching the play of thoughts. Opening fully to the grief of losing a beloved is another. Embracing the suffering of any being on the edge of formlessness is a third. Feminine knowing aligns itself with the breath of the universe, of the deep rhythm into and out of form. Feminine wisdom is the fruit of that deep knowing from within.

These two ways of knowing—masculine and feminine, objective and subjective, mind and heart, detached and engaged—work on two different levels. Neither is superior to the other, and both are jewels of knowledge and consciousness. In your society, only masculine knowing is recognized as valid. This profound one-sidedness results in skewed outcomes, visible in the realms of education, relationships, cultural values and public policies.

Some of this is rooted in fear. There are skillful practices to address fear, which in turn can facilitate the emergence of more feminine ways of knowing, or perhaps better named as "sensibility."

I must add here that I have never liked dichotomies. I think they obscure more than they reveal.

She laughs. Yes, you are quite right. Dichotomous thinking is a core practice of what we are calling masculine inquiry. And you are right to consider it inadequate. We are really speaking of something much more fluid and complex. We will try to give you some better language for describing other ways of knowing. For the time being, hold two other metaphors in mind: a continuum, with masculine and feminine inquiry at its poles; or a multi-layered scheme, with multiple weavings in and out, interpenetrating each other.

Dichotomous thinking calls forth objections and opposition. That is not helpful here. It becomes difficult to discover new viewpoints or to pry open cracks for more inclusive and complex realizations. Dichotomous thinking narrows one's access to reality.

Compassion and Suffering

Compassion is not all "sweetness and light." It is not the mother comforting a child with a scraped knee. It is not the cup of water offered to a thirsty person or alms to an outstretched hand. These are virtuous acts, but they are not the core of what is named compassion. So, our first task is to rescue the word "compassion" from its centuries of sentimental overlay.

Compassion is fearless. Compassion is fierce. Compassion denies nothing and withholds nothing. Compassion ignores social conventions and rejects polite courtesies. Nothing is more radical than compassion. It is a quality of awareness more than any specific activity in the world, though it can fuel a thousand kindly acts.

Compassion will seize you by the back of the neck and shake you hard, to break through the torpor of everyday mind. Stripped of your fictions and fantasies, you will stride into reality with new eyes and new heart. Only this can truly be named compassion, and this is the straightest path to radical freedom.

Compassion and suffering are parts of a single whole, just as inhaling and exhaling are parts of a single breath. Imagine compassion as a being coming into form, and suffering as a being dissolving out of form. That raises a profound question for you: if this is the very nature of being, why would one half of that cycle be suffering? Who suffers what? And does it have any purpose?

First, let's consider only sentient beings, beings with some rudimentary neurology. Rocks and planets also come into form for a while and then dissolve, but they are not sentient in the way we define it here. All beings come into and dissolve out of form, but not all forms are beings. We wish to speak about beings here.

Why do sentient beings suffer, when their form begins to dissolve? With form comes boundaries. In some ways, form **is** boundary, and within those boundaries there is a center of sensation, simple or complex. That center of sensation—a small bundle of nerves that can initiate motion, for example, or search for food—recognizes what is within and what is outside that boundary. And that is the most elemental definition of a self, with no implication of self-consciousness or self-awareness. A self, then, is that center of sensation that can distinguish between what belongs within the boundary of the being and what does not.

Remarkably, beloved Teacher, that is also the basic definition of a state: the center that claims boundaries, decides who may be within, and protects them from those who would violate those boundaries.

She laughs. Yes, exactly. And that center of sensation is, or should be, the political leadership, the "head of state."

The first task in a simple being, an amoeba, for example, is to identify nutrients to ingest and to identify dangers to defend against. It is protecting its form, and thus, its life. That is its goal and purpose. But we must be careful not to impute human dimensions of consciousness in simpler beings. "Purpose" is a particularly tricky word. After all, to be in form is what the amoeba is to do, and it does what it can to continue to be in form.

But eventually, it cannot. It is unsuccessful, and it dissolves out of its form. Does that amoeba suffer? Well, we really don't know. But we do know that it tries to avoid its own dissolution, so we can say that it wishes to continue in form and it expresses its preference for a long life. In that we have identified the simplest sign of suffering: dying, despite a preference to live.

Moving up the evolutionary ladder, that "preference to live" fuels increasingly complex patterns of perception and behavior. In human beings, the ego supports the preference to live, and the center of sensation has evolved into the human brain. Sensation, neurology, cognition, language, and speech developed along the way. Everything is organized around the primary task of staying alive: discriminating boundaries, bringing in what is needed, and keeping out what might be harmful. It is the same work for a single cell as for you: staying alive. Beings in form intend to stay in form. And when they cannot, they suffer.

May I ask a question, please? His Holiness the Dalai Lama always teaches, that of course, we all experience pain, but that suffering is a creation of the human mind. Suffering is an addition to pain, which seems to intensify or prolong it. I think he would say that all beings experience pain, but only beings with minds like ours really suffer. Are you arguing something different?

No, but that is a good question. The difference lies in the language. I don't distinguish between pain and suffering as he does. I use "suffer" to mean exactly what he means by "experience pain." He is surely correct to point to the enormous differences between most sentient beings and a few others, most obviously human beings, whose minds allow them to remember, imagine, amplify, and associate mentally. It is those mental capacities that can add suffering to pain or create it in the first place.

All sentient beings wish to remain alive, and so, all sentient beings suffer. Only humans realize they will disappear, and the consciousness of death dyes human life with its strong colors. Yet being born and dying, taking form and leaving form, is **the** central reality of living organisms. How do we reconcile these two things: the certainty of death and the powerful instinct (for it is an instinct) to stay alive?

It is only a minor exaggeration to say that all of human culture—social institutions, economic arrangements and cultural activities—is an attempt to manage the certainty of death and its implications. While those cultural practices may assuage for a while the second order of suffering—the fear of death—none resolve the issue.

The only resolution is to reframe the perceptual framework of being in form and recognize the universal rhythm that is the fundamental pulse of all material reality, from amoebas to galaxies. Can humans come to embrace both form and formlessness? Can you calm your anxieties about death?

That may sound like a metaphysical question, but some ease with dying and death is necessary in order to become a vehicle of compassion. Released from the obsessive avoidance of formlessness and of constantly securing one's boundaries, one can open to compassion: the potent, powerful energy of compassion, not its weak shadow.

This is the deepest wisdom not only of the Buddhists, but of many other spiritual traditions as well. Each has had explorers—men and women of mystical, contemplative, or sheer radical instincts—who have found their way to these insights. Those who have returned to share something of what they had discovered have left you suggestions for starting your own journey.

Remember now your original question: what is the dark face of compassion? It is the calm awareness of the finiteness of forms. It is only ego's view, that this is darkness. But it is not so. Light streams from a heart calm in the face of formlessness.

Opening the Heart Center

Compassion and suffering are woven into the fundamental structure of the material universe, and consciousness must respond to the ebb and flow of form and formlessness. Opening the heart center within is part of that process of awakening, and it increases the flow of light into the human world.

Compassion and suffering are aspects of consciousness—not the dimly lit awareness of a simple, sentient organism, but the expansive and self-reflective consciousness of a human being. Human development is rooted in the long processes of biological evolution, but that does not mean that human consciousness can be reduced to some neurochemical activity in the brain. The great arc of human development is much more complex than that.

Compassion is a response to suffering, either one's own or someone else's. The movement of compassion begins with attention, noticing another's difficulty or pain. The suffering must be perceived and acknowledged, before a response is possible. Compassion will begin to flow when the intention is to alleviate the distress. The first decision allows the perception of suffering; paying attention and responding then follow. At each point it is possible to close your heart, to ignore the suffering, and not to respond.

What encourages a person to make the choices that lead to a compassionate response? The great religious and ethical traditions agree, you must be taught. A child learns the ethical rules of human life from her parents, her community, religious teachers and texts, and even through reason and self-inquiry. "Do unto others as you would have them do unto you." But clearly this has not been sufficient. There are many explanations: self-interest, fear, laziness, lack of imagination, lack of resources, limited energy, or simply human nature. Each can be overcome by one thing: a lively, alert, and well-nourished heart center.

The heart center is really an organ, perhaps the central organ, of a human being. It equals the brain in its potency and complexity. Not taxed with the tasks of regulating the body's biological and chemical processes and keeping them in equilibrium, the heart center's perception is powerful and deep and sensitive to a much broader range of energies than the five senses of the brain. It is the organ which can access the realms of Spirit, of the Teachers, of dreams, and of soul. It is how a human reads emotion, bewilderment or fear in another. It is the vehicle of intuition and hunches and of deep memory and inexplicable equanimity. It receives visions and speaks in symbols. It is never satisfied with the obvious or the superficial, but always probes more deeply, below the appearances of things.

The heart center, as the source of feelings, if untethered to the mind and careful thinking, can go far astray. It can wallow in the fanciful, the false, in gossip and superstition. It can even organize harm to others, believing it pursues some good. Mostly it is a perceptual capacity with the power of insight and intuition. And it is the essential vehicle for deep and steady compassion to arise. There is no other way to perceive another's suffering and choose to ameliorate that suffering, without in some way leaning upon the heart center, as atrophied and weak as it might be.

How then do we uncover the heart center and begin to nourish and strengthen it? One uncovers the heart center by peeling back the many layers of fear accumulated in this and previous lives. The heart center is nourished by exercise. It needs access to people with stories, to poetry and theater and song, to the many expressions of human depth and struggle. Opening to the deeper dimensions of those around you strengthens the heart center and reinforces your confidence in its perceptiveness and decisions. You uncover and nourish your heart center by clearing away old defensive layers, through humane education, and in the tumble of relationships.

The heart center opens by breaking open; for example, through experiencing some great grief or loss. The crucial word here is "experience." In that verb is hidden a deep teaching. Anyone who has known a great loss and felt the waves of grief roll in and out like some terrible tide knows how the heart center can break open. And anyone who has not will find it difficult to peel off enough protective layers so she can access her heart center. But there is no shortage of causes of grief! So, there is always material at hand, not least the profound fear of death, which accompanies every human being.

The first impulse for many is to shut down and push the grief or suffering away. This is the moment of denial and deflection, of re-naming or turning away. Fear fuels that response, for grief can seem overwhelming, a kind of death itself. If someone, however, can stand still and allow the powerful emotions to enter and she can allow herself to experience them fully, it can become a moment of profound transformation. Rather than adding more layers over her tender heart center, she agrees to experience the grief, and that allows her heart to open. She breathes into the great pain, and then softens under it. This requires courage and a sturdy self-confidence in being able to navigate one's own depths. It is a critical decision-point, which must be revisited over and over.

Sometimes the grief or suffering is so great that there is no "decision point," no moment when you can choose whether or not to allow the painful emotions in. A normally well-defended person can be astonished at the emotional devastation and how it can upend a previously well-regulated life. Though it hardly seems so in the moment, this can be a great gift. She has arrived at the charnel ground within, with fears and terrors scattered about. The stronger the assault, the deeper the medicine, the deeper the release, and the wider the opening. This is blessing, profound blessing, but it arrives in the guise of a wrathful deity. That leering face of terror, dripping with blood and gore, is the healer, the cunning opener of the heart center. This too is the Dark Goddess, beloved student, doing her necessary work with her intricate tool kit, peeling open the buried heart center.

Why is this necessary? It gives birth to great rivers of compassion and kindness. Which is to say, of course, that it unites the person with the flow of the universe, with all of life, and with the deepest wellsprings of meaning, however that story is told in the end.

If there is no great grief, how can she find her way to that river? How does she open her heart? How does she agree to open to suffering, hers and that of others?

That, beloved student, is the work of every religion. Religious practices, rituals, and traditions are instruments of this great work. Religious narratives have at their core a story about suffering and compassion, death and new life, human limit and human expanse. The tools lie all about you, ready at hand. Teach your students to pick one up and become expert with it. Practice opening the heart center to what is. Notice the fears that would prevent this. Do the disciplined, patient work of dissolving fears. The heart center emerges naturally from this work, gaining energy with each step.

There is no need to "talk yourself into" compassion. Compassion flows naturally through the opened dam of your heart center. Break the dam and compassion flows. Your next choices are where to direct it: to those nearest? Fine. To those far away? Fine. To yourself and your unhealed parts? Fine. The more compassion flows, the deeper its channels. It goes to where it is needed; it heals those it touches; and in the process it heals the suffering and woundedness of the compassionate one.

Compassion and Consciousness

The flow of compassion through the heart center also supports the expansion of consciousness, and vice versa, in one of the most blessed cycles of all. Once that bodhisattva cycle is launched, you can simply relax into it and let it carry you into the very heart of the world.

In the last section we spoke about the relationship between compassion and suffering, and how ultimately they are two facets of a single aspect of reality, the complex rhythm of form and formlessness. Later we described the opening of the heart center and that as a person's heart opens to another's suffering, compassion flows through that heart with ease. This becomes then a powerful, positive cycle for the student on her spiritual path.

In this section we will describe the implications of this positive cycle for consciousness. And in the next we will return to the original question about gender, of Noah's wife and how she might have responded, if any had been willing to listen, to the call to build an ark.

Though this is an intricate mental and neurological process, it is useful to understand better how the practice of compassion stretches consciousness. The intermediate term, of course, is the heart center, for compassion as a response to suffering is the work of the heart center. One perceives suffering, truly perceives it, not cognitively but through the heart center. As we described earlier, the heart center is a powerful organ of perception. This is not well understood in Western studies of anatomy, physiology, perception or cognition. It is also an emotional muscle, which becomes more powerful with use. That is why every religious tradition offers religious practices meant to exercise that emotional muscle to generate more generosity, kindness, cooperation, and peacefulness.

As the heart center is exercised, its perceptiveness increases and its ability to respond appropriately (itself, a definition of compassion) becomes more acute and generous.

Is this directed by the ego? Not really. It works most smoothly when it nearly circumvents the ego. It's the heart center's opening which fuels the expansion of awareness, and in many instances it supports radically new consciousness. The ego has not been able to obstruct this responsiveness to others, nor limit who might be a legitimate recipient, so consciousness expands quickly. The ego, if not undermined, is at least sidelined. We will also want to compare cognitive and heart center approaches to awakening. This is especially pertinent for a North American audience because so few of you understand the critical role of the heart center and its role in perception, compassion, and consciousness.

Focusing on the needs of others can discipline ego, even while relying on ego's ability to focus and pay attention. Ego is not to be obliterated, only disciplined. It is essential for certain purposes, but it cannot be allowed to define the moment, describe the situation, or undermine the outcome by plucking the strings of fear and mistrust.

Who is it, then, who stands aside and shapes ego's role? What is the name of that part of the person?

That is the Self, the animating core of a person, an impossibly complicated word. Neither East nor West fully understands what it means to speak of "Self." Self is this particular incarnation's version of Buddha-nature, the fundamental core of the person, the indestructible intersection of Spirit and individual, which is also the template for maturity and enlightenment. It is how each person embodies an aspect of the infinity of Spirit. It is that part of the person that cannot be destroyed, only hidden or deflected or ignored. It is why every person, regardless of their actions, can be welcomed into the circle of metta, into the circle of kindness and concern. It is why no person can be excluded from compassion. And this leads us to consider the intimate relationship between compassion and consciousness.

The Intimate Relationship Between Compassion and Consciousness

Imagine this, please. Take as a spiritual practice looking for people whom you would not be willing to include within your circle of compassion. Identify what they did/thought/said that makes you unwilling to gather them into your circle of care. These are the rejected outliers, abusive male relatives on one hand or genocidal political leaders on the other, and many in between.

Focus on one. Try to look at him or her with curiosity, and try to understand something of her motives, her inner disabilities or fears, her history. Try to imagine possible causes of the egregious behavior. Gradually and mysteriously, you will notice a softening in your chest. That initial curiosity made room for kindness. There was then room for thought free of judgment. Something slowly opened.

In a light-handed way, please experiment with this. The most difficult cases are often the near ones, not the horrifying slave owners and dictators and murderers. The near ones have left their marks on you and your beloveds. Though this might seem counter-intuitive, it is with your personal relationships where the stakes are highest, and where the aching need for letting go into compassion is the greatest. The victim is near, perhaps even yourself, and the need to be free of that anguish is excruciatingly clear, even a matter of sickness or health. Remember, the purpose of this practice is to become aware of where you balk and why. Those are the instances you will want to investigate further. What is the history? What is at stake? What is buried there?

This practice can also be a powerful solvent on fixed ego positions. By looking for the places where there is no natural inclusion and working backwards to the ego position, it is sometimes possible to identify the blockages. This is a very powerful tool to be used with, yes, you guessed it, great compassion for yourself. Beware of your vulnerability to emotional overload. This strengthens the heart center while limiting ego's ability to interfere. The muscle of the heart center stretches and stretches, while ego's fears and denials are held at bay. Not silenced but held at bay, also with compassion.

So, I must ask my question again, beloved Teacher: who stands apart and holds ego back, while bringing the heart center more fully into play?

She laughs. Yes, that is the question, isn't it? It is she who listens so carefully to me, fluently bringing my Teaching into language and then writing it down for others to read. It is that acutely focused, wide open aperture of an entire person, like a telescope's lens of many small mirrors gathering up the vague signals from outer space and focusing them into a coherent image. Then your cognitive mind, which ego loves to claim as its own, wrestles it into language and writes it down. Ego is everywhere in this process, but never in charge; it is never the sole lens of perception or interpretation. It is tricky, this little ego; one cannot live easily with it, and one cannot live without it. It is an essential tool of consciousness, yet the danger lies in its claim to be the only source of authoritative and reliable knowledge. If you believed ego's claim to primacy, you would never recognize the crucial role of the heart center. That would be a great tragedy. It has crippled your society and culture, as we have described many times.

Opening the heart center fuels the expansion of consciousness; it supplies the energy needed to push out the boundaries, do the very difficult work of discernment, and assists with the life-long task of managing ego. Let's look at those one by one. Many life events can expand the boundaries of awareness: a terrible shock or loss, an illness, a profound disappointment, a piece of art, a strong creative experience, a rich immersion in nature, and a thousand other moments. When the mind is ready and able to stay present to such an event, great change is possible. It can deepen its understanding, dissolve a foolish assumption, or receive a rush of creative insight. Much religious training, especially contemplative practices, teaches the student to hold still and actually experience her experience. It sounds simple, even foolish. However, it takes diligent practice to be present in this way, especially in the face of a deeply unpleasant experience.

Discernment is more subtle and challenging, as it requires a blend of cognition and heart openness. Ego must be allowed to function here as the tool of focused mental attention, but it must partner with the deeper perception of the heart. Discernment weighs the two "knowings," both masculine and feminine, so it can evaluate and integrate new information. This provides the guidance necessary to choose the best response. At the same time, it expands her field of awareness as it leads from perception to discernment, and then to decision.

How does this process assist with the task of managing ego? Ego has been yoked together with more complex forms of perception and discernment, and so is unable to launch its claim to primacy or to block information from other sources. Ego has not been obliterated. Even if it were really possible (and it isn't, except through drugs or severe mental illness), it would not be desirable. Ego can focus a flashlight on a particular problem, for example, and bring to bear related information. The most skillful approach partners the ego with other forms of perception and values. A partnered ego is much less likely to grab the keys and make a run for it. Better for the whole family to go for a drive!

As we return to our larger theme, the relationship of compassion and consciousness, there is one more point to discuss. Ego is rarely the source of compassion and kindness; it is not impossible, but it is difficult. The filters of ego self, competitiveness, self-absorption, and seeing others as objects are powerful obstacles to the easy flow of compassion.

But in truth, a steady, strong flow of compassion is actually a fundamental part of human nature. Kindness, nurturance, and protection of near kin is deep in your neurology. Your brain's first task is learning to distinguish between the good "others" (your mother or caregiver) and the less good "others." As they mature, people do extraordinary things on behalf of those they care about, because every human has a profound capacity for compassion. The tasks are to remove the obstacles that block it, on the one hand, and on the other to expand the category of "good others." And here "good" means: worthy of my care and compassion.

Most in the Buddhist and Hindu worlds of South Asia recognize this quality of human nature. People in your world, the people of the Book, do not. Before practicing opening the heart center, expand your own circle of care. When everyone can be considered kin, everyone can be included in your field of compassion. The Dalai Lama often teaches this in the West by reminding his listeners that every being was once your mother. Unfortunately that often alerts the psychologically tuned Westerner to a frightening reminder of childhood difficulties, rather than a prompt to care for everyone. But for all human beings, Western or Eastern, the real work is dissolving the obstacles to the natural flow of compassion.

It seems then that we have reached the heart of our current human predicament. What teaching could help us do exactly that, so we might feel refreshed and encouraged in the great work ahead of us? What could help us retrieve our sense of our shared humanity and begin building a world which could house us all safely and securely? We must navigate what Joanna Macy calls "the Great Turning," and we must do it very soon. Surely this is the key to that, its essential practice.

You are already underway in the "Great Turning," as she so wisely names it. It is difficult to see, because you are in the midst of it. And like Marx's Owl of Minerva, who only sings at night, after the events have been accomplished, you will not fully grasp the enormity of the transition until it has reached its fullness. You and your colleagues won't see its fulfillment in this lifetime, but you will surely return and participate further. Glean the small signs now; put your ear down to the ground to hear the gathering choruses of voices; and trust that what you are coming to understand is also realized by countless people around the world. Please keep searching for like-minded colleagues; send out your messages and reports; and make connections wherever you can. Make the World Wide Web a living network of people around the globe. This must be your vision, your hope, your strength, and your delight.

Fear, the Heart Center, and Compassion

We've come full circle as we remind ourselves that fear is at the root of the closed hearts, the paucity of compassion, the cramped consciousness, and the reign of ego which so characterizes your world.

The prime obstacle to the flow of compassion through the heart center is fear. The energy of fear fuels competitiveness, greed, selfishness, disconnection, and aggression. Fear reinforces stubbornness and ignorance, isolation and self-pity. Fear exaggerates vulnerability and ignores cooperation and mutuality.

The fundamental fear, which lies at the core of all fears, is the fear of formlessness. This includes not only the fear of one's own death, the irrefutable fact of life, but the related fears of formlessness and impermanence: changes in social arrangements, livelihood, close relationships, and further out, changes in the broader landscapes of political and economic life. If you dig down a bit you will discover the intense human desire for predictability, to control outcomes and avoid change.

None of this is "bad" or to be regretted. It is wired into the substance of being itself, including humans. Other species must respond to changes in their environment; only humans can change their environment, purposefully or not. Altering their environment to serve their own purposes, humans have now so changed the planet that it may soon—in no more than a century or two—be unable to support human life as you have come to know it.

How could this happen? Essentially, because of human giftedness in observation, experimentation, imagination, creativity and organization. Humans have practiced these gifts for millennia, as well they ought, for they are powerful and precious. But at a certain historical moment, let's say, the late European Middle Ages, they pushed the fruits of the human heart center out of the public realm and confined them to those small parts of community and private life called "religion" and "ethics." The heart center played an insignificant role in the great movements of the Enlightenment—the development of science, modernity and individual rights.

Wonderful to recount, in many parts of the world the gifts of the heart center have been invited back into your community life. As an organ of perception, it recognizes the dangers of the radically manipulated environment and proposes ways to pull back from the abyss of species self-destruction. You are beginning to hear the call: humans must recognize their complex interdependence with each other and all other species. To fathom this revolutionary idea, one must disentangle the structures of individualism, competitiveness, materialism, and consumerism. Human nature must be reimagined. All this would assist you to plumb the depths of human fears, and start human society on its long path of healing.

And there is a hidden prize. Working through these obstacles to clarity about the human situation and creating new ways to organize human life automatically begins the release of compassion. Dissolving widespread hard-heartedness, especially within powerful institutions, can release immense creativity and vision, for there are indeed other ways to organize human societies and economies.

Everyone who joins this revolutionary process—as an individual making a life choice, as a citizen, a worker, an educator, or a policy maker—will make an impact. The old arguments about the contemplative vs. the active life dissolve here, as do the tensions between "working on oneself" and tending to one's neighbor. Every intentional act can feed the "Great Turning," the unimaginably huge and complex shift of the species life of the most complex organism in your world. To be an active, conscious part of this is an extraordinary privilege, and on most days it should fill you with joy.

Multiple Paths, One Destination

I have been thinking about the powerful awakening of consciousness that can follow opening the heart center. If that is truly the path of compassion, is there any other path to greater consciousness?

Buddhist teachers have discussed this for centuries. Some have argued that the path of compassion, which itself is closely related to the path of devotion, is the surest route to awakening. Others have argued that the path of wisdom, of profound study and deep meditation, is the most reliable path. In our view, everyone is both right and wrong.

First, both paths lead to the same destination. That is extremely important to understand. Both result in dethroning the ego, allowing the practitioner to recognize her Buddha nature, her fundamental enclosure within All That Is or Great Mind. You might name it the realm of Spirit or Radiant Heart.

Second, because each person must find her own path, which suits her personality, history, and temperament, it is excellent that there are two paths, which lead to the same destination. And within these two families of paths are many variations. Finding the right path can be an arduous life task all by itself, especially in the West now with its extraordinary variety of teachers and practices. This is a great contrast with the traditional way, when a student studied with a teacher from her local monastery. But even within a single monastery there would be followers of various paths and sub-paths, each with a different emphasis and relying on its preferred texts and practices. Even though there were and are intense doctrinal and philosophical debates—a core practice in some lineages—few would argue that there is only one way to proceed. The great Himalayan tradition has always recognized that different types of students might need different practices and texts. And so it has always been. This, by the way, has facilitated the ease with which Buddhism has taken root in so many different settings.

You are a good example. The first big text you received from your Teachers, *What in the World,* begins with an analysis of cosmic energies and ends teaching about love and compassion. It sits squarely in the wisdom tradition. You found it energetically more challenging than this text, which focuses on opening the heart center to allow the flow of compassion. The path of compassion and devotion resonates with who you are and is your natural path.

But please remember, eventually every student must integrate the insights of both mind and heart, of wisdom and compassion. That is brilliantly illustrated in the Buddhist and Hindu world by the union of the male deity with his female consort. And thus must it be, for the union of wisdom and compassion reflects two aspects of the singular perfection of the human being, the realization of her Buddha nature.

Gender and Compassion

One last question for now: why do so many cultures around the world express the embodiment of compassion in such gendered ways, highlighting the feminine and feminine energies and perceptions?

This is a difficult analytic problem, for we must consider cultural understandings and practices while we simultaneously try to peer underneath those cultural constructions to something more fundamental. Is it psychological, biological, or even anatomical? Once you could grasp the deep pulse of cosmic energies into and out of form, you were able to realize how profound your question was. But still, there is confusion in your mind, as these moving parts don't settle into a clear, stable pattern.

Let's separate the question into its parts. First, women nurture, and men act. Women care for the home and family, and men go out into the world to create institutions, economies, and, they would claim, culture. They create boundaries around territories, which introduces conflict, aggression, and violence. Men become warriors to enforce the boundaries and protect their women and children. This ancient gendered division of labor marks very early cultural practices. When it is embedded in a narrative explaining its mythic origins, it has become the forerunner of modern gender relationships.

What began as a division of labor and later of spaces led to a deeper claim about gender: that women and men are fundamentally different kinds of human beings with vastly different capacities and skills. The ability to conceive and give birth, originally an immense source of respect, much later would be reduced to an inescapable liability. Women were confined to a lesser form of human body, and from that emerged countless inhibitions and prohibitions. That is still visible today.

To justify this increasingly unequal gender system, ever more elaborate theories were created: religious, psychological, philosophical, anatomical, economic and political. This is the world you grew up in; critical analysis of gender and its institutional and individual practices and explanations became the work of your generation. There is more to do, but there has been a stunning awakening of women around the world as a result of this sustained cultural and social critique. It continues to detonate, with profound consequences.

We are brought back to the dichotomies of thinking/feeling and mind/heart so characteristic of modernity, each with its gender valence. Men do science, and women do early childhood education; men practice medicine, and women nurse patients. Those conventions are shifting in response to powerful forces in your society. It is no surprise that many people now wonder what characterizes a whole human being.

Once it made sense to identify the core of each gender role as a reflection of biological and psychological capacities. Now most thinkers dismiss that as essentialist thinking, though current empirical research suggests it may be much more complex than first seemed likely.

Yet those pairs of opposites, such as thinking/feeling and wisdom/compassion, are still identified with gender, as quintessentially masculine and feminine. If we strip the dichotomies of their gendered names, as the liberation movements demand, do they still reflect some basic difference between the sexes? The debate will surely continue, as will the uneasy gap between contemporary understandings of gender and the traditional practices, which identify compassion and honoring the heart center as feminine.

This is especially acute now, because of the hegemony of science-based empiricism in your society. There is little space for the practices of compassion. Women resist being confined to a narrow and undervalued gender role, and it requires great courage for men to ignore the classic prescriptions of masculinity and claim compassion as an essential personal value.

If you cannot re-situate compassion at the center of your culture, bound intimately to wisdom, you will fail to rescue global human society from self-destruction. You may name it "reclaiming the feminine" or "healing the environment" or "erecting boundaries around global capitalism." But the work must be done. Human flourishing must be the core purpose of the emerging global society, not economic growth and corporate profits. The "Great Turning" is no longer optional. It must be realized in all domains: political institutions, health care, education, family life, cultural practices, spirituality, economic activity, the arts, and so much else.

For that to happen, individuals must unearth their own capacities for both wisdom and compassion. Every person, male and female, must explore his or her own heart and heal its woundedness; each must identify and defuse defenses and fears. The most revolutionary work available right now is to uncover, heal, and dissolve one's own deep fearfulness. Potent fears, unconscious and unacknowledged, fuel the destruction of the Earth's carrying capacity for human life.

The first exercise of compassion, then, must be directed towards oneself. With that enhanced understanding of one's own life comes the beginning of wisdom. Suffering then can be acknowledged. That sounds so simple, but it is not. It is hugely challenging for modern people to recognize the depth of their own suffering. Here, there are no gender differences, for the gender system, which so compresses the possibilities of a fully human life, has afflicted everyone, men and women alike.

It is a tremendously exciting moment to be a human being, for this is the first moment that self-compassion, self-acknowledgement, and self-healing are culturally and psychologically available to more than just a few. This, by the way, is one reason so many beings chose to return to Earth for a new life at this historical moment. The opportunities for vast expansion of consciousness and wholeness were so attractive. In earlier times, only a commitment to an intense spiritual practice could lead to such deep understandings of the self. Spiritual teachers, known and unknown, have followed this path. That explains the remarkable similarities at the heart of the world's great spiritual and religious traditions.

Now, with the flood of easy global communication, many more people have access to these ancient traditions for cultivating knowledge of the self, wisdom, and compassion. No longer is it reserved for a tiny, mostly hidden elite of exceptionally developed and privileged people. This should be cause for great gratitude and joy.

There is another cause for gratitude and joy: so many of you hover on the edge of despair over the terrifying crises you see facing your world. But each crisis carries within itself a stunning opportunity—for more awakening, for dramatic shifts in global consciousness, and for new practices of cooperation and collaborative problem-solving. A century or two from now, a cultural historian might write that this moment was as momentous as discovering the uses of fire or the possibilities of agriculture. It is no wonder that so many of you feel lost and discouraged, because it is impossible to grasp the nature of this transformation while in its midst.

When I began this project several years ago, I was looking at images of Tara and you, Kwan Yin, and wondering what lay behind that deeply compassionate face. Then I realized that the faces of the great bodhisattvas in human form, such as Thich Nhat Hanh, the Dalai Lama, and Archbishop Tutu, also imaged compassion for me, so like the famous photograph of Lincoln at the end of the Civil War, with his face ravaged by suffering and compassion for his countrymen.

Yes, when you have seen that human face of compassion, you can imagine the face of the deities, the bodhisattvas not in body. You recognize them through their energy. We without material form are countless, and most of us have recognizable energetic patterns. Some of us can communicate easily across certain boundaries of this vast cosmos. In most communities there are some highly developed humans able to connect with these Beings, directly or indirectly.

Humans name these Beings and their communications with them according to their religious and cultural traditions. That accounts for the variety of gods and goddesses, religious practices, cosmologies and theories about human nature. Yet, if you plumb these cultural practices deeply enough, you will begin to discover, underneath the cultural "clothing," remarkably similar content. There is an irreducible core, which humans intuit, experience, and rely upon. Many students want to know that core, especially if they feel unsatisfied with their own tradition. They want to peer down well below the surface .

That makes me think about Jung's concepts of archetypes and the collective unconscious.

Yes. Let's pause here and consider his work for a moment. Jung's postulate about archetypes and their central place in human psychology is helpful, but it blurs, however, a difficult problem: where is the boundary, if there is one, between the individual psyche and the realm of the non-human? Jung, deeply committed to his public identity as a scientist, never published his most radical thinking about these questions. Yet a careful reading of his later work reveals that he wasn't at all certain. If the collective unconscious is essentially unlimited and without boundary, as well as inaccessible to ego consciousness, it would seem that he is pointing to a vast nonmaterial reality. We might echo contemporary physicists and name it a parallel universe.

These archetypes, numinous and powerful, express potentiality. They are a persistent pattern of energy, a non-material being, if you will, or a non-material center of energetic relationship. It is difficult to express in language.

To say it slightly differently, a deity is an archetypal form emerging from a persistent pattern of energy, usually from another realm, and able to project its energy in a way that humans can sense or receive. Various cultural and religious traditions then give that central archetypal core a legible form and identity. Narratives and meanings accumulate around it, often until it is so heavily encrusted with cultural material that the numinous is completely hidden.

For example, you understand that Tara, the Blessed Mother, and myself, Kwan Yin, are all names of a common female deity archetype. It gives form to the compassionate feminine, which nurtures life. She is sometimes engaged in agriculture, human fertility, and other dimensions of reproduction and renewal. The variety of associated cultural practices does not diminish their potency or meaningfulness. This is one reason to protect diverse cultures from the homogenizing pressures of modernity and globalization.

She can be a powerful source of energy for human devotees. Every human, consciously or not, longs for care and support, so this archetype also receives powerful projections from people in need. It can provide a deeply meaningful energetic opening, which can even lead to a relationship with that archetypal pattern of energy, that Being.

It seems to me there is some kind of extraordinary cosmic alignment under way at this moment. Let me try to put what I am slowly intuiting into words.

First, powerful, new energies are pouring into the Earth community, challenging all of us to open to their potency and possibilities.

Second, the long exploration of masculine energies, of focused ego consciousness, of science and invention, seems to have hit an end point, at least for the moment. Its destructive qualities seem to challenge science's contributions to humanity.

Third, we are watching waves of political and social energy to improve the lives of women and girls. Do we finally recognize that the other half of humanity must be brought into every realm of human endeavor? Some argue there will never be peace until women are at the negotiating table. Others argue there will never be ecological balance until the perspectives of women—and the feminine aspect of men, always to be included—set agendas and insist on new parameters for human life.

And fourth, there is a remarkable expansion of human awareness, especially at the grassroots level. Individuals assume responsibility for what has always been the work of synagogue or mosque, church or parliament. It is named civil society; it is named the dialogue between local and global; it is named the great awakening of individuals around the world. Manjushri described it so memorably in What in the World, *with his image of "lights turning on around the globe."*

It seems to me, and I know you will correct me if I don't have this quite right yet, that underlying all of this is a great flow of compassion toward all beings and the well-being of our planet. There is an urgent desire to reduce needless suffering by competing less, manipulating less, and demanding more for those of us less well off. This, I believe, reflects the dramatic opening of the heart center in so many people, giving them energy and commitment to make a more humane world.

Slowly, that compassionate outreach is joining up with the profound insights of wisdom, of what is possible and imaginable, what living in balance with the natural processes of the Earth would look like, and how we might create that reality for ourselves and all beings here with us. In a sentence, then, and again I am struggling to put this into language, powerful new energies are releasing the archetypal feminine more fully into the world, allowing feminine-infused compassion and wisdom to emerge into its rightful place in the human community and allowing us then to pull back from the brink of catastrophe and self-destruction.

Yes, yes. Exactly. Let me add a few notes to your summary. First, women must place themselves in these critical conversations at negotiating tables and policy-making processes around the world. And they must courageously speak as women. This will shift the outcomes of those meetings, and it will encourage men to engage with their own feminine aspects and come into better balance themselves.

Second, the integration of compassion and wisdom happens on many levels. Compassion opens up awareness of needs, especially to relieve suffering and injustice. It invites wisdom to help it create appropriate responses. This partnership of compassion and wisdom is the most radical form of social action; it has never been more accessible than now, when the liberation of women coincides with the exhaustion of modernity. Compassion and wisdom must be activated on every level. Each person must develop an open and vibrant heart center and join it with an acute and fearless mind. And what is done by individuals on this path must also be brought into the community. No community can reckon with and release its fears until a critical group of individuals in that community has also done that serious fear work. This actually can initiate a very powerful dynamic, for as the community recognizes its fears and how fears obstruct its ability to enhance its well-being, it can provide powerful support for individuals to undertake their own challenging fear work.

The Dark Face of the Compassionate One holds fear in her gaze and in her embrace, allowing the fear to soften and dissolve. As we have taught you before, there is always the suffering attendant to coming into and out of form. That is inescapable, most especially living in a material world and within the parameters of time and space. But that suffering need not be encased in layers and layers of additional suffering generated by fear. That is the work, which the students have volunteered for, if I may say it that way. That is the work of waking up, of expanding consciousness, and opening the heart center and mind to the reality in front of you. And that is the place of maximum freedom to be fully human.

This is what we wished to say to you about gender and compassion. You and all the students are always in our care, whether you are aware of it or not. That is the reality of the cosmic flow of compassion, which is also the pulse of the energy of the cosmos.

Part III

Walking the Path

Introduction: Guide to the Path

We begin now the core teaching on opening the heart center within and accessing the cosmic Heart Center. It must begin with suffering, for it is suffering that turns our attention towards our most essential selves. It is there we must look for healing, for meaning, and for the deepest reality we as human beings have access to and are part of.

By necessity, these chapters must lie in a neat row, one after another, as if to insist, there is a path, a logical order or at least a real-life order. But it is not so, truly, it is not so. There really is nothing linear whatsoever about engaging with the mysteries of Spirit and waking up. The student goes forward, then comes to a halt. She will return to an old issue, once again, and then lurch forward. So, these chapters do not suggest a well-marked, continuous path. That does not exist. Consider them rather themes you are likely to encounter, over and over. Each visit will deepen your understanding. Nothing is ever wasted, truly, in the long work of healing heart and mind.

Each of us recognizes that we suffer. Buddhists have made this their specialty, and I am thankful for that profound tradition's relentless focus on it. The teaching is remarkably simple: Lean into the suffering, become familiar with it, and watch it carefully. Breathe kindness to it and to yourself. Watch it shape-shift.

But executing this turns out to be not so simple. It turns out to be merely the prelude, an invitation to a stunning voyage of self-discovery and self-healing. On the way, that self seems to fade away, transformed in surprising ways. There will be countless repeats, turning back, missed signals, side trips, losses, confusions, and refusals. I can attest to this, as you will find in some of these conversations with the Teachers and their patient attempts to help me finally get it. I have not yet arrived at "finally," for sure. But what follows here, in Part III, are the instructions I have received and continue to practice. Both Kwan Yin and Manjushri have blessed me with numerous conversations full of advice on how to bring the sometimes abstract Teachings about suffering and training in compassion and wisdom into the very concrete messiness of my daily life. Some, like how to break open a dream to find its kernel of new truth about who I am, became tools I have used nearly daily. Others, like learning how to lean into suffering and confusion, rather than try to do an end-run around them, took a very long time to learn and then to remember to use. One quiet goal has seemed to be to help me see my life and my relationships more accurately, with less projection and less illusion about what is and isn't real. Another purpose has surely been to support deep healing of heart and mind, often through the morning reminder from Kwan Yin to breathe kindness to myself. Exhale, she will say, and again! I laugh now, because every student of mine has received the same advice from me at some point! There is humor everywhere, wry jokes and teasing, for this business of being fully human is well, just a bit crazy-making some times! And laughter is the most potent way to undermine a preening ego, believe me.

Last is fear, that deep current which shapes so much of my life and of human life, everywhere. The whole path could be named: living skillfully with fear or releasing all unnecessary fear. The Teachers urge us all to heal our fearful selves, for only then will we be able to build the human communities we would wish to live in. To heal our fears, personal and collective, and not just repress or project them onto others, is a lifetime of patient work. I now grasp how it requires understanding its fundamental rootedness in human life—the metaphysical context of the Teachings—and the most intimate healing of a person's spirit, in its most personal form.

To help you navigate, I've noted the principal writer (or two) for each essay, but please remember that I have been embraced in these relationships, with their subtle and explicit conversations, over many years. Some times it has seemed to me that it all flows out of a single stream, and that in the end, an essay's particular author no longer matters very much. Please take what you need, and leave the rest. Circle around your own Spiral Path, attending to advice as seems helpful. You too surely have a Teacher and Guide, whether talkative or not. Trust that guidance, and be glad. And don't forget to exhale, a lot!

I'd like to give you a glimpse of the profound healing I've experienced from walking this path over many years. Kwan Yin summed it up for me one lovely day in 2016 on a sand dune next to the Atlantic, reminding me of the enormous power of skillful re-framing of old issues.

Learning to Reframe: Five Great Sorrows and Gratitudes

Kwan Yin

Primary for you now is the absence of deep partnership, a life in a couple with a heart beloved. You have mourned this and sought to remedy it for many years. It is time to lay it down, to call off the search.

The second life-long sorrow is how you have felt it wise and necessary to hide your soul and its vibrant, green, life-pouring energy. This has been the cause of great hurt to you and your well-being. That this is your soul is cause for gratitude. That you've had to hide it is cause for sorrow.

The third great sorrow is how you've thought it necessary to silence yourself, to shrink yourself, and to deny your gifts and powers. Again, the qualities are cause for gratitude, and your need to hide and deny yourself are cause for sorrow.

Your fourth great sorrow is your caution, your resistance, and your native skepticism over the reality of Spirit acting directly in your life. You have prayed to be released from that inhibition these last years, and so it will be. This too is cause for both gratitude and sorrow.

Your fifth and last great sorrow concerns your physical well-being. Now you fear you will not complete your work before you die. There have been years and decades of acute and chronic ill health, which has prevented you from doing many things you had hoped and prepared for. You have borne this with steadiness and grace, but it has been a deep and abiding sorrow. It has also been a transformative teacher as well, and so, a source of both gratitude and sorrow.

Fear: An Introduction

Penny Gill

Underneath suffering lies fear. So, we will begin our long journey on the Spiral Path with a first Teaching on fear, followed by numerous Teachings on fear as we proceed.

We must first remember how fear underlies so much of what longs within us to be healed. We return to where we began, years ago, in the first book from Manjushri, *What in the World Is Going On? Wisdom Teachings for* Our *Time.* There Manjushri teaches about fear, and how it has shaped our lives, communities, and world.

There are two kinds of fear. The first kind, communicative fear, we share with many other species; it gives us information about an immediate danger in our environment, which requires a response: flight or fight, in most cases. This superb mechanism, sensitive to "the tiger in the grass," vastly enhances our survival, and we can only be grateful for it. The second type, imaginative fear, however, is created in and by our own minds. It may or may not be grounded in external reality and may have little connection with any plausible threat to our survival. Yet it can just as powerfully repeatedly shape our perceptions and our behavior, until it becomes an unexamined dimension of our supposed reality. Because it is wound so tightly with human intellect and human imagination, its roots are much more difficult to trace. It is a delicate process to uncover those deeply rooted fears and begin the long and hard work of dissolving them.

The steps of this process, however, are simple and straightforward. First, identify the fear lurking deep in your heart and mind. Give it a name, and as best you can, bring it up to the surface. Then, greet it with kindness and understanding, over and over, day after day, until it slowly dissolves. It will lose its power to trigger a sense of danger, to initiate a counter-attack, and to escalate a situation out of all proportion to its worldly significance and heft. You will be rewarded with much more ease in your life. And the violence in your community and world will surely be reduced, no longer fueled by your fearfulness. It may seem too small to make a difference, but truly, it is the best way to begin to heal the generations of fear and violence in the United States.

Fear underlies, like a solemn *basso continuo*, each topic that follows. Fear creates and maintains Shadow. Fear blocks access to the heart center, which dries up the source of kindness and compassion. Eventually, you will doubt the very reality of a non-material realm and the world of Spirit. A life so desiccated and shrunken is barely human. The consequences of unchecked fear are incalculable.

Healing fear restores well-being and opens new opportunities for expanding consciousness. Since consciousness is the purpose and meaning of human life, attending to your fears and becoming familiar with your unconscious material is a powerful way to live a fully human life.

Without fear, we would all be stuck in the Garden of Eden, unaware of the perfect pleasure of our lives, profoundly stupid, actually, and ignorant of reality. Praises be for fear!

In the first Teachings gathered in *What in the World*, Manjushri showed how fear underlies human societies, initiating the development of organizations, political and economic institutions, social and religious practices, and much more. At the end of the book you will find the argument that the most powerful healing of fear is to address it with compassion and loving kindness. All this is true.

Here, however, Manjushri addresses fear from a different direction. Fear shuts down access to the heart center. An excellent way to approach that is to investigate Shadow and its contents. For our purposes, perhaps a better term for Shadow, in this context, is all the aspects of a person that could be integrated into a fully whole self. "The stone which has been rejected will become the cornerstone." That is well said. Shadow is a great gravel pit of rejected stones.

Let's remind ourselves that Shadow is the repository of all that the emerging small self, ego, cannot embrace about itself, or that the child has been told cannot be accepted as part of her. This is how a child and a young person learn to be an acceptable member of their family and their community. They must agree to the rules and regulations, the assignments of status and privilege and duty, and the larger meanings, which shape the cultural practices and the daily instructions about how to speak, eat, relate, imagine, and interact with others. From the unlimited potential of a newborn child, pieces are identified and discarded, until the desired person emerges, who will fit nicely into her local world. The discarded bits are then swept up and stored in the Shadow. That newly emerged person will have to haul that great sack of rejected pieces of herself around for the rest of her life. It is fear which keeps it all in the sack, and it is fear which forces her to haul it with her wherever she goes.

A person's first rebellious act is when she stops and says: Why? Why can't I say that, do that, be that? She has walked out of the Garden. Now she begins the long journey of becoming fully human.

The forces of repression are great indeed. Fear takes many forms, concrete and threatened, physical and emotional. Underneath all lies the drive to survive. Survival— physical, emotional, social, spiritual—can all be threatened. Resistance requires courage, vast amounts of courage (yes: *coeur*, courage, heart). If the first yes is followed by a second yes, and then a third, the strengthened heart brings more energy, clarity, and understanding of what is at stake. This was the gamble of leaving the unconscious stupidity of the Garden of Eden and embarking on the path of consciousness—the longest journey of any species. And its glory. It will be worth everything. With these first thoughts in mind, let us turn to the grand project of becoming a fully human being.

Learning to Lean Into the Dark

Penny Gill

Darkness—or pain and suffering—is the universe's great curriculum in wholeness and grounded sanity. The darkness corrals the untethered energy of high cognition and forces it to reckon with limit, with obstacle, with uncertainty, and even with mystery. Our first experience of darkness may be its randomness, when a terrible loss or tragedy suddenly arrives, unanticipated and unannounced. We shriek: What is happening? Why is this happening to me? What have I done, to deserve this? What does it mean? We want it to "make sense," to carry some meaning in its great paw. There will be meaning, but only when we make right relationship with its pain and how it has dislodged us from our usual lives.

My mother and I struggled my entire life over how best to relate to the dark and painful events of our lives. She believed fiercely that the smartest way to respond was to tune it out and ignore it if at all possible. Deflection came next, then re-naming if that was appropriate, and then, if all else failed, denial. Repeated, firm, self-congratulatory denial that something so sad or hurtful could possibly have happened. And then, carry on.

Even as a young child, I found it maddening, and I would insist that I really was sad, or that someone really had been hurtful. She could ignore the child dramas of a tough day at school or a bully in the neighborhood as well as the life-altering heartache of losing my father in the war or my severe illness as a young adult. Because she couldn't admit the enormous impact of those events, it was nearly impossible for her to respond compassionately.

I began to wonder about compassion, which would lead me to

this path and ultimately to this book. For this is how this whole project began.

One soft June day I was nursing a deep heartache of my own, sending kindness to my sad self and feeling a subtle, sweet connection with everyone in the world suffering the same thing, at that moment. It was as if I were holding something precious in my hand, a many faceted jewel, and in each facet I could see the intricate interrelatedness of suffering, attentiveness, kindness, and compassion. My heart had opened completely naturally to the suffering of others in that moment, apparently triggered by my awareness of my own suffering. In that instant, I recognized that acknowledged suffering opens the gate to compassion. I wondered then, perhaps compassion and suffering are not so different, but actually, two sides of a single reality. If compassion is rooted in kindly attentiveness, an open face reflecting an open heart, then suffering must somehow be the other side of that compassionate face. And thus, I was invited to pursue my own winding journey into this mystery.

As a youngster I came to believe that there was much more reality in the dark side of life than in the supposed light, all-is-well version. I have no idea how I came to that conviction, but conviction it was, and a firmly lodged one. It seemed to me much firmer ground to stand on, as well as a more realistic view of how other people were likely to behave. It is perhaps no surprise that I chose to study politics, especially Europe's tumultuous twentieth century. There was more than enough incomprehensible darkness there to try to wrap my mind around. My favorite authors as a teenager and young adult also wrestled with the disastrous catastrophes of modernity: Marx, Mann, Rilke, Hamsun, Jung, Simone Weil, Merton, and a host of others. Later, Eckhart, the Cistercians, the Hebrew prophets, Bach, and contemporary Buddhists such as Thich Nhat Hanh, Pema Chodron, and the Dalai Lama would join my mental and spiritual world. Each peered into the abyss of human nature and Western civilization and struggled to wrestle some meaning out of their interface.

Suffering, of course, offers itself to us as the great teacher. Rarely, I suspect, are we able to respond very fully. It is just too hard, and the obstacles seem to stretch out endlessly. It is overwhelming. A long story stands behind that precious moment when suffering and compassion, heartache and relatedness, showed themselves to me as facets of a life-giving jewel. My hope here is to try to tell some of that story, so that you too might receive that insight and, like me, find yourself changed.

I have learned that you must gradually strengthen that little heart muscle that allows you to show up and be present to suffering, yours and that of others. Start with yours, because in your own experience, your responses can be tentative, or subtle, or way off the mark, and no harm will be done to another. The first step is to cease the automatic denial or deflection that we each have been taught, by the relentless exhortations of our society.

You must also learn to notice a dart of emotional pain or a sudden ripple of unease on the surface of your feeling life. Well into my thirties and well established in the early stage of my academic career, I found it nearly impossible to recognize what I was feeling, or even to know what that meant. I knew I wasn't happy, because why else would a person begin therapy? I knew things were somehow not right in my life, but I couldn't name any good reason why not. I had a wonderful job at a splendid college teaching terrific young women. I was in a relationship that seemed rich and nourishing, and I was able to live not far away from work surrounded by woods. I had good friends and interesting colleagues. I had just gotten tenure, and I felt pretty firmly planted in my life for the very first time.

Remarkably, though I had received a superb education at Northwestern and Yale, I couldn't report a *feeling*. Years later I would come to understand that it was precisely my fine education that had so successfully excised emotions, feelings, and subjectivity from the curriculum, the classroom, and from acceptable scholarly inquiry. One could study other people's emotions, but the emotions were then an object, usually an object of pathology. Perhaps it is no wonder that undergraduates create escapes from this rigid mind-set in the form of alcohol, drugs, and other risky behavior—unskillful ways to capture and intensify emotional states.

Just because social scientists and the academic world had exiled human emotions and whole-hearted subjectivity didn't mean that they disappeared, of course. Pushed below consciousness, they went underground, to be stored in perpetuity, like nuclear waste. But repressed emotions do not have a half-life. Instead, they gain in virulence and potency. It is no wonder we instinctively resist opening that cellar door to explore all that has been rejected and repressed over a lifetime. But if we do not open that door and begin to reclaim our feeling life and our Shadowed selves, we will never be able to live our fullest human life. We will surely be unable to create a more sane and humane society, and we will be unlikely to halt our destruction of our civilization and perhaps even the life of our species. Not to be too grandiose about this task!

It was long and slow work. A piece would suddenly surface, often triggered by a current problem, and I would have to turn my attention to its resonances and echoes, to identify what else had been activated. An irascible colleague at work would lose control and subject all of us to an incoherent harangue, and for days I would feel on edge. There really was no physical danger, but it felt like it. I wanted to make myself small and inconspicuous, at the same time I wanted to shout back with long, perfectly argued rejoinders about his stupidity. I learned to ask myself: who does he sound like? Where am I, when I fly into that dimly visible space? When I finally recognized that he echoed my stepfather, I learned to say to myself: "My irascible colleague is not my father. I do not have to stay in this room. I can keep myself safe." Tone of voice had catapulted me back thirty years. I could move back and forth identifying shouting arguments and emotional textures. Some of those habitual responses were perhaps appropriate for a small child. I needed some new ones suitable for an adult in the workplace.

This was the first step of what I call "exercising the small heart muscle to be present in the face of suffering." A thousand repetitions later, the swamp is still not drained. I am grateful, however, to be more skillful.

What does the darkness require of us? Like the *Phantom of the Opera*, the darkness requires we acknowledge its reality and its presence in our lives. But beware: it is no phantom! The darkness is not only "real," but it is potent and consequential. The less the acknowledgement, the more powerful its impact. Let that be a warning. Consult the opera if you have any doubts.

We believe the darkness is disfigured and ugly. It cannot be allowed out in the daytime, for it would horrify others. One of little ego's major tasks is to constantly remind us of this, because it claims to protect us, especially from revealing ourselves to others.

To begin to heal the darkness requires that little ego take some time off each day, and in its absence we can introduce ourselves to all within that has been rejected and sent away. Curiosity and courage are all that is needed to begin this process. The first encounters with these unfamiliar parts of ourselves may be painful, but eventually a safe form emerges. Discovery and encounter are possible, and we find that there is no catastrophe. Instead, you will begin to receive the gift of some unfamiliar aspects of yourself that had been chucked away with the rest: a lost capacity for intuition, for example, or a rich imagination, or an irreverent streak that sees into the heart of things. How splendid to retrieve and welcome these new pieces of who you are!

This will give you courage to head back in and look for the deeper layers, where childhood despair and family wounds lurk. There is no joy in unlocking this door, only profound grief as you recognize the ancient burdens you have carried all these years. You wonder, how did I manage to get an education, care for the young, and make a life for myself? What would my life have been like without that deep soul injury? I could hardly bear the pain of that or the anger lying underneath it.

This process of unearthing the deep layers of woundedness and recovering the grief and anger may go on for many years. Each time that I have thought, "Now, I have finally gotten to the bottom of this, and there is no more," I am brought back to the work. Perhaps I will never finish this recovery work, only this life's portion. I don't know. I am puzzled that it can take a lifetime to undo the conditioning of just a few years of childhood. The child's brain and heart are so receptive and undefended that foundational patterns of perception and relationship resist transformation. But I learned that acknowledging the darkness and what is lodged there eventually brings relief and healing.

To not acknowledge what has been lost or rejected from the conscious personality may result in a conventional, superficial life. Or, it may release deep rumblings and torrents of tumult. Surely that underlies some of the widespread dysfunction in our society today: substance abuse, the pandemic of violence, and the mindlessness of so much American culture and public life.

I don't understand why some are called to descend into their own darkness, and some are not. Karma is a handy explanation, but that just pushes the question back to previous lives. I do know that it is no fun, especially at the start, and resistance is certainly "rational," in a certain way. There are no awards for walking down that dark Spiral Path; indeed, it is more likely to be met by others with ridicule and condescension. So, I hold it as a mystery, without doubting for a minute that it was to be my life path. There have been times when I was considered gloomy or even depressive, because of what I was unearthing. To integrate the new insights and energy takes its good time, as well. Speaking or writing about these descents was even more difficult. I often wondered if anyone else would find these stories helpful. In the end, what seemed so dark and so challenging to my visible life turned out to be life-giving, struck through with light and meaning. And even more wonderful, it opened a door to streams of compassion.

I have come full circle. Learning to be present to my own deep suffering, or even to the simple hurts and bruises of every day life, has become my practice. I'm more skillful at recognizing my emotional terrain. I try to remember to pause the automatic responses and slow down my reactivity; there is space for compassion to arise, for self and others. For compassion is rooted in attention, in recognizing what is actually happening, within and without.

Opening to our own heartache, current and historical, allows a free flow of kindness and compassion. Really, nothing more needs to be said. That deep practice of self-care helps me to stay grounded, which facilitates the flow of energy to others. It is an old saying, that to change the world, we must first change ourselves. Healing our own heart shapes the tool for changing the world. The more we can open our hearts, the more of the world we can embrace.

The deepest healing often requires the kindly attention of another. We are all hard-wired to be in relationship, which fosters this profound growth and honors our fundamental interdependence with each other. In my mind's eye I see you, my reader, longing for encouragement and companionship on your journey. You call forth my words, and I bow in gratitude.

On Suffering: The Door to the Heart Center

Manjushri

The heart center within can only be opened through the path of suffering. This is a very hard teaching, and we will try to make it clear to you. You know this through your own experience, obviously, but it is not so easy to discover the deep patterns, which underlie that. We will begin with that now.

The energy seems very heavy.

Yes, indeed, it is very heavy energy. The sorrows of the world, the deep need for self-protection, the fear, which underlies it all, yes, it is heavy indeed. It is not easy to be a human being, to live in a body and be subject to the tight constraints of space and time and mortality. There is profound wisdom in the first noble truth, that you human beings, and all beings in body, suffer.

No being wishes to suffer. It is not surprising then that they develop tools for minimizing suffering or escaping it altogether. For beings without much consciousness, these tools become their survival strategies, and they shape the course of evolution in a most wondrous way.

But for beings with the seed of consciousness, such as yourselves, this instinct to avoid suffering brings some complex challenges and consequences. The seed of consciousness is the sense of "I." The sense that "I am." This is the nascent ego, which will ultimately become the small self. And she, ego, begins to fashion tools for diminishing suffering or eliminating it completely. This becomes, in your world, medicine, science, central heating, air planes, and much else, as we have discussed with you several times.

Over and over throughout her life, a child is taught to reject and hide those parts of herself, which are not welcome in her family and her community, and instead, to nourish and identify with those parts which are acceptable to those upon whom she depends. This is called socialization; it is the universal process of bringing a child into full adulthood with membership in her community, her tribe, and her world.

For some, this is an easy passage, especially if the young person's abilities and insights mesh smoothly with the values of her world. But it can happen sometimes that there is great friction in that interface between child and community or even between what is welcome in her person and what has been rejected. In some, that friction becomes the inescapable irritant, which will initiate the journey towards much wider consciousness.

The valuable core remains, literally the heart of the matter and indeed the heart of the person. What has been rejected by her world, and so consigned to darkness by the growing child, must be uncovered, retrieved, and re-integrated into her larger self. Only this process, difficult at best, can mitigate the second round of suffering, that which she has experienced through the negative judgments of her world and her fear of them and their threatened consequences.

This, as you know, is no easy task. At first, you feel great heaviness in your limbs, barely able to move through the day. The layers of self-protection resemble iron shields strapped upon the struggling body. When you peer down into the darkness and see what covers the wretchedness, you are overwhelmed, even terrified. And surely discouraged. How to even begin to enter such darkness, much less penetrate it? The story of the grand quest has begun, though whose it is or which path is not yet clear.

Let's pause, then, in our story, until the seeker arrives. What triggers this journey in a person? What rouses a person to even ask the question — why am I sad? Why am I discouraged? Why does nothing seem valuable or important or even meaningful?

We, the Teachers of human beings, recognize the answer is suffering. If anything can help a person begin this journey, it is suffering, pain, heartache, and despair. And you human beings in your villages and communities have developed powerful tools for responding to suffering: mental and emotional suffering, the suffering of loss and death, and the suffering that comes with an "I" and a sense of self. Suffering, however, responded to wisely, can vastly expand consciousness.

In your culture's foundational story of Adam and Eve in the Garden, nothing happens, for there is no truly human life and no consciousness, until they recognize they are naked. The snake and the apple are simply devices to reveal the movement of their minds. That moment of self-recognition—oh, I am naked!—is when the human story really begins. This is when the main characters arrive in the story.

It is centrally significant, though rarely commented upon, that the moment of awakening to a sense of self arises from being seen, from being acknowledged by the other. In this case, of course, it is the man and the woman recognizing the presence of God/Yahweh, the great "I AM" of the whole story. Immediately they also recognize their own reality, their own presence there. Consciousness is born out of relatedness. No single, solitary human being could become fully conscious. Even a hermit lives within a dense matrix of relationships. A simple reading of the Noah story suggests that the animals board the ark "two by two," in couples, presumably to be able to reproduce when they return to dry land. Well, perhaps. But that other foundational story points to the necessity of relationship. The pairs loading onto the ark suggest that the new, post-flood world will be a world of relationship, and so its human inhabitants will also have the potential for consciousness. The ultimate "work" of the Earth and its people will be consciousness. The universe at play is a universe, which intends to become aware of itself.

Think backwards with me for a moment: from the desirability of consciousness to the necessity of relationship; from relationship to a sense of self. From the socialized self back to the child taught fiercely what is and is not acceptable in her world. From that process of child education to the unavoidable division of the child into two parts, acceptable and unacceptable. Layers of impenetrable material accumulate over what is unacceptable until it is invisible and silent, hidden away in the darkest, most remote corners of the person. Each layer added to reduce the child's fear of rejection turns out to increase the child's suffering.

The usual human response, then, is to add another layer in hopes of masking that suffering. That layer might be more denial, or it could be more activity, more whiskey, more compulsiveness, more greed, more attempts at control, or even more violence. Human beings have discovered many ways to self-medicate that inner suffering from the rejected self and the imbalance and hungers of the acceptable self. Most of you die this way, having lived only a tiny bit of your potential wholeness. That is truly the human tragedy.

However, a few, brought to their knees by their pain, turn instead toward the pain. Why they do this is a mystery, even for us. They are often old souls, if not old people, and have already learned that adding more defenses does not solve the problem. It was to answer this very question that many early cultures created the concepts of karma and reincarnation or other stories of healing and redemption.

There is a mysterious moment when a person leans into her suffering, rather than trying to subdue it or turn away in hopes of easing the pain. It may be a human capacity, but it seems quite rare among you, especially since the advent of modernity with its thousand ways to supposedly mitigate suffering.

We note here that every great religious tradition offers a central teaching about human suffering. It often includes a cosmic or theological explanation, as well as practices to embed the suffering in a larger context of meaning. Though these still serve the needs of some devotees, the vast majority of people alive today remain untouched and disconnected from these religious narratives. That is a major reason for the explosion of self-medicating practices so common in your world today. The culture of modernity denies the reality of non-material realms or energies. It considers Spirit to be a foolish fiction of the imagination. The experience of suffering then can only be met on a material or non-spiritual level. None are really helpful.

Suffering is the door to the heart center, the only door. It is the very last place one looks for relief and healing. That turn, which goes against so much of human culture and socialization, that turn *towards* one's suffering, rather than *from* it, is the great key to all that follows. Jesus understood that. The Buddha understood that. Confucius understood that, and Lao Tzu. Thich Nhat Hanh and the Dalai Lama and

Thomas Merton and all those named as the "holy ones" and the "great teachers" all understood this. That is precisely why they could become the teachers of their communities.

Why do some recognize that door, while so many others don't? Souls must try many other doors first, lifetime by lifetime. An old soul has known many failures, many unsuccessful attempts to find ease and comfort in many previous lives. It seems to us, that it is the life-tempered old soul who finally surrenders to the ubiquity of suffering and mostly out of curiosity, if not desperation, turns toward it. What is this experience? You all know it. None of you are able to prevent it or escape it. What does it teach you about reality?

These questions unlock access to the door. And the long journey of healing then begins. The instruction, then, is to hold open that door just a bit, to allow a glimpse into that darkness. Just stand there, until you become fully aware of what you have just done. It is revolutionary, and it must be recognized, before proceeding. Then consider the critical question: will you agree to the path of transformation?

Agreeing to the Path of Transformation

Manjushri

Why is it heroic to undergo transformation, or even to agree to a transformative experience? There are several ways to address this. First, and probably most significantly, all organisms prefer stability and predictability. If their systems are already in equilibrium with their environment, there would be an energetic cost to any change. Since the fundamental principle of matter is to conserve energy, resisting energetically costly change is the default strategy. Energy spent in pursuit of food, shelter, and reproduction is expected to conserve or gain energy. At an organic level, there is a built-in conservative bias to avoid change, if change will cost additional energy.

Some animals, especially mammals and even birds, will play. Why do we mention that? Because it would seem that play goes against that fundamental hard wiring to conserve energy. But play is a form of practice for more serious tasks, such as self-defense, or exercising the neurological and muscular components of flight/fight or mating.

It is not until we consider the primates, especially human beings, with their greater cognitive and imaginative abilities, that we find complex reasons to pursue voluntary change. Let's pause for a moment at "voluntary." No being is immune to involuntary change: light, temperature, availability of food or shelter, territory, predators, rain, and a thousand other aspects of life on Earth can require accommodation from an organism. If there is no adequate response, the being will suffer and/or die. Only higher primates, and especially human beings, can choose change or even actively seek it. Some seem to require change, as if it is an appetite or need. We think of humans searching for a new experience, a new mate, a new place to live, or new food. Perhaps these preferences for novelty reflect the pursuit of pleasure, but that doesn't tell us much about the pursuit of transformation. It is more likely an attempt to re-establish an equilibrium of desire, attention, and satisfaction. Still, it is unusual for a human being to agree to or even seek out transformation. It requires an override of the deeply instinctual resistance to change; energy is to be used frugally.

Agreeing to transformation also requires imagination and social practices. Imagination is the great human ability to pose a "what if?" It allows for creativity. We consider imagination to be the critical difference between human beings and all other sentient beings. As we have taught elsewhere, it is the human gift of imagination that gives rise to so much fear. It has stimulated the extraordinary diversity of human cultures. The basic elements of play have given impetus, through imaginative activity, to the creation of story and ritual, on one hand, and to the arts and modern science, on the other.

Now, perhaps, we have a first answer to why a person might choose to pursue transformation. With imagination operating, she can think things could be different. Perhaps, then, she becomes receptive to some trigger, some subtle invitation. It could begin as simple curiosity. Or, it could be she is out for a walk, meets a stranger, hears an unfamiliar bird song, trips and falls, or gets lost. We might wonder if perhaps some deeper part of her has initiated this process, in order to lead her to the next phase of her life.

A person suffering something deeply painful can be persuaded that change could ease that suffering, and so might be willing to try. There are many ways to choose change in hopes of re-establishing an inner balance. Easing suffering is the most common motive for people, while a strange or accidental trigger for a journey of transformation is more common in stories, especially fairy tales and myth. These ancient stories seem to recognize that change will lead to more consciousness, while the real-life person seems to believe the change will lead to less suffering and more ease. The fairy tales probably have it right!

Now we can explain why agreeing to the process of transformation is heroic. It requires a person to choose change, to undergo what will enable that change, and agree to a certain degree of surrender. She will have to give up some power and sense of control. This is named heroic in every culture, because to voluntarily give up control and autonomy on behalf of some unknown value, not even certain the bargain will hold, is to override one's fear of change. This challenges the fundamental rule to avoid unnecessary change. It's a gamble to bet on an unpredictable outcome, especially having surrendered one's usual modes of self-care and protection. A person's normal mental economy would consider it a crazy thing to do!

Or so it seems to those standing by and watching, especially for those living in a culture focused on the satisfaction of desires, real and manufactured, and where the consumer reigns supreme, though never satiated.

But nothing in the modern arsenal of responses to discomfort will work, as each is meant to stop or block the suffering. It is the central teaching of the Buddha, the Awake One, that suffering is inherent in life, and that the causes of suffering—mostly arising from change and impermanence, which manifest as loss, illness, and death—can be fruitfully examined and even embraced. This is not a masochistic view, but a deeply intelligent direction to pursue.

The first step is to interrupt the belief that suffering can be avoided. Then you must face the impulse to flee or suppress the pain. This is the main purpose of meditation, especially the practices of mindfulness. That restless mental activity slows down, and instead of fleeing, the person learns to sit still and notice what is happening. "Oh, ouch, that person's comment really hit me hard!" or "Oh, I'm scared of this, that I won't do this properly. I'm not any good at this." Or "My dearest beloved is gone. How will I live?" If you can stand still in that moment, breathe, notice what is happening, and at least briefly interrupt the automatic responses, you are on the path.

This then becomes the practice: a couple times a week, then a couple times a day, and then, many times a day. It takes perseverance, but that is no surprise: you are re-routing neurological and emotional pathways that have been reinforced over lifetimes. Eventually, this practice brings you to the door of your heart center, as we have described earlier. As you stand there, considering whether or not you wish to embark on this strenuous and great journey, gather up your strength, your curiosity, your little basket of hopefulness, and whatever small shards of trust in the universe you might still have stashed away somewhere. Stand there, then, and choose to open the door to your heart center a tiny crack.

Opening the Door of the Heart

Manjushri

You have worked very hard to excavate layer after layer of old hurts, sadness, wounds, grief, and anger. Between those layers lie layers of fear, defenses, repression, and denial, all silenced and pushed down as far as possible from your conscious self. You have peeled each layer back, seen it and its roots, and employed some skillful means to name and heal it, and then let it go. There you stand, in front of your now accessible heart center, and your feelings can now move easily, without obstruction.

Paradoxically, letting that buried pain go turns out to be very difficult for some people. We see they are fiercely protective of some of those deep wounds, not to avoid their pain, but because the pain might still serve some purpose. It can carry meaning, as well as legitimate a life narrative about how things came to be as they are. Old pain, held closely, can buttress a basic identity.

Let me try to explain that more fully. Perhaps if I use the word "victim" this will make more sense to you. If a person identifies herself as a victim of some wrongdoing—an abusive or absent parent, a betrayal by a caregiver, a wrongful conviction, or the loss of a beloved person, for example—that sense of having been victimized can become a central aspect of an identity. The psychic or emotional injury can provide a powerful explanation for current difficulties at school or work or with relationships. "I was hurt so badly by X, it is no wonder I am unable to perform, relate, take responsibility, or live without substance dependence." The seed of identity as victim is nourished each time such a thought is offered to oneself or to another; pretty soon it becomes indispensable. Over time, more and more of one's life and surroundings and even of one's personality are woven into this burgeoning system of identity.

There is a cascade of refusals: a refusal to allow the original wound to be healed; a refusal to let go of the identity as victim; a refusal to take risks, to grow, and to venture out into troublesome or unknown territory; and ultimately, a refusal to take responsibility for one's own health and well-being. The person has succumbed to fear (and using the passive voice here is precisely correct). She becomes immobilized, barely able to enjoy any moment or undertake any project. Defenses pile up, layer after layer after layer.

This is why the universe smiles kindly at a person who is so brave as to face the fear, the hurt, and the experiences of powerlessness and vulnerability, and who chooses instead to lean into the suffering and become her own physician. It calls upon an uncommon courage.

Or desperation? I think I have only been able to make this turn when all other options have failed, when the heartache simply has worn down my resistance, as if there is nowhere else to go or nothing else to try. I guess it is an odd kind of surrender.

Yes, that is helpful. Ego or the conscious self is flooded with emotional discomfort to such an extent that the old methods of dampening it down no longer work. The misery so intensifies that there is no way to escape. In this overwhelming moment, an unknown aspect of the self says: Whatever can this be? Go look more carefully!

Then the energy begins to shift. As you say, one leans into the suffering and peeks into the darkness. The work has begun. We have entered the seeker's journey, that central myth of all time. It is the story of confronting the great danger and discovering its true nature.

How does someone turn toward their suffering rather than try to leave it behind? What disposes someone to realize that her heart can be healed and the heart center approached, that its suffering can be eased rather than suppressed, and that there can be new life? For this is the beginning of the great spiritual journey. She glimpses that the only way forward is to drop below the surface, to turn towards what seems inaccessible, and to enter that dark unknown. That is the beginning of the story, both of the myth and of our Teaching about healing the heart center.

What starts the person on her path? The simple answer, which you well know, is misery. Despair, hopelessness, frustration, failure, loneliness, or meaninglessness. Why is this the case? Because each of these undermines ego's claims to have it figured out and to know the ways of success and power and safety. Ego of course does not know these things, but only claims to know, and when that becomes clear, ego loses its credibility and power. Ego's energy drains away, leaving exhaustion or depression in its wake. At some point the only possible stance is surrender: "I can't do anything about this, so I guess I simply must endure it." Ego has been dethroned, and there is nothing left to do. This is a sacred moment.

The purpose of the journey is to make contact with the very core of what constitutes a person. Different cultures and traditions name that differently: soul, spirit, core Self, Buddha nature or Atman. It can be silenced and ignored, through personal ignorance or misuse, social or political pressures, or great personal catastrophe. But it cannot be eliminated. It is the deepest mystery of Being at the heart of every living creature, but its most complex form is in human beings. It is that to which you bow and say Namaste. It is how Great Mind or Cosmos or Source manifests itself in a human life. It expresses a single intention: not ease, not success, not knowledge, but awareness, greater and greater awareness and consciousness. The spiritual journey is taken on behalf of awakening this greater consciousness. Wisdom and compassion intermingle here, healing heart and mind. This is the universal spiritual journey.

Every sacred ritual and religious tradition addresses this journey. For those still embedded in their own religious upbringing, following its path is a fruitful choice. For those moving towards other traditions, or none at all, which is an increasing number of you at this moment, re-telling that ancient archetypal myth may offer helpful guidance.

The journey begins when a suffering human being ceases to turn away from or repress her pain and finds herself standing still in its presence. Many questions arise then: why is this happening to me? What is the matter with me? What can I do, to diminish this pain? Does it [illegible] any purpose at all? What is a life for, and is it worth this?

[illegible]efore we proceed any further, it would be helpful to clear up a [illegible]es about the hero's journey as a map of the spiritual path. The classic Western version tells the tale of the hero, almost always a young man, and his tribulations during a descent via a journey underground. He may meet strange beasts and great challenges on his way, which often culminate in a terrifying confrontation with a great danger, sometimes appearing as a vicious dragon. The hero must slay the dragon, rescue the treasure and return to his village, laden with gifts.

This myth outlines the work of a young man on his way to adulthood. He is still embedded in "Mother," that powerful feminine complex, and he must claim his autonomy from both the complex and perhaps his earthly mother as well. This map to male adulthood, as it has come to be in your society, valorizes ambition, competitiveness, autonomy, and self-reliance. It is meant to solidify that emerging male ego, made firm in its rejection of the feminine and perhaps imaged as a bloody conquest with a magical sword. This is the archetype, which undergirds male dominance and privilege. And it raises the question, in its one-sidedness, where is the feminine, especially the Divine Feminine?

Is there another way to read this myth and rescue it from itself, so to speak? Yes, indeed. Suppose we consider its protagonist to image ego, the conscious personality with which you all identify. Then, when that small conscious self finally surrenders to the great spiritual journey towards healing and wholeness, as we have been discussing it here, the task that emerges is to gain access to that core Self, the deep Heart, or Soul, name it as you wish.

For the little self, which begins the journey, slaying the dragon of cowardice is an appropriate task, as are swords, subterfuges, miraculous escapes and wounded dragons. But if the journey is to make contact with the central Self or Soul, to encounter the Divine Feminine, then the dragon is certainly not to be slain! For Soul's purpose is always to integrate lost or hidden aspects of the person. The dragon is a split-off or obscured fount of energy, and it must be recognized, welcomed, and brought back into the widening circle of the conscious personality. Soul's task, when it is in body, is to gather up the broken pieces, the shards from previous lives, the rejected and the abandoned remnants of lived experience, and integrate all that into its rightful orbit around the core of Spirit. Soul's task is the divinization of all that has fallen away from its proper relatedness with Spirit, with the Sacred. This is the true journey of the seeker, and it leads to profound wholeness, healing, and awakening.

In this way, the hero's journey or the seeker's underground journey reflects the archetypal myth of healing and awakening, lived out through many lifetimes and on many levels. It follows its Spiral Path, circling around and around, until all is healed and functioning freely and fully. This is Jesus harrowing hell during His archetypal three days between death and new life. This is the core human experience underneath all the stories of transformation, death, and rcsurrcction.

This is the deepest story of your life now. It is how the Shower of Spirit initiates new consciousness within a particular life. *What in the World Is Going On?* maps this on several levels: the individual, her community, and her world. It launches the journey, makes fear visible, and then leads the person towards healing and new consciousness.

The Outer Journey: On Pilgrimage

Manjushri

I had recently returned from a two-week pilgrimage with a group of friends to Lindisfarne and Iona, two ancient destinations for pilgrims in Scotland. It had been a challenging trip for me in many ways. Had it been of any value for my own spiritual journey? I asked Manjushri. "Can pilgrimage—an outer journey—also serve as a path of inner transformation?"

Yes, of course. Pilgrimage has multiple meanings and purposes, so it is not so easy to generalize. It is fundamentally a spiritual practice, which honors some aspect of the religious tradition within which it and the pilgrims are embedded. Going to Mecca or Jerusalem or Boudhanath immerses the pilgrim in the grand narrative of her tradition. The extra effort, both physical and financial, intensifies the pilgrim's commitment and proclaims to both self and others, the significance of her religious life. Pilgrimage is both an individual and communal affair, which reinforces identity and meaning. It is a highly visible way to say, "My religious beliefs mean this much to me!" and it bonds the participants, known and unknown, in deep and powerful ways.

Pilgrimage removes someone from their normal life, with its obligations and habits and identities. Stripped of family and social roles, she is more available to her fellow pilgrims and strangers along the way. The heightened dislocation and vulnerability can support an opening to inner transformation as well.

This is how pilgrimage and the journey of transformation can resemble each other. Not all pilgrims, especially those traveling in a group, will embark also on the inner journey, but certainly, some do. The strangeness of the pilgrimage, all by itself, can cause inner distress or offer moments of profound questioning of oneself and one's life.

Sometimes people may feel a raw disquiet or an urge to embark on a pilgrimage, without really recognizing why or how. The psyche itself may suggest pilgrimage as a way of initiating radical self-inquiry, without the person understanding its source. There is just a sense, "Well, I just really need to do that!" This is a sentence you have heard from friends planning the long walk on the Camino.

There is another form of pilgrimage we should mention: visiting a particular sacred place, such as a grave, a spring or well, or a place of healing or ancient ritual. The impetus may be as simple as paying devotion or a prayerful request for healing, wisdom, or plentiful rain.

A life responsive to Spirit is often a life sensitive to place, and places of rich energy marked by shrines or prayer flags offer the pilgrim a meaningful destination. Pilgrimage addresses both time and space in powerful and mysterious ways.

Paradoxically, perhaps, pilgrimage can also offer solitude, even traveling in a group. The very strangeness of it all, plus opportunities for anonymity, can invite sustained introversion and introspection.

There are other similarities. A pilgrimage can be dangerous to life and limb. The pilgrim really is intentionally pursuing uncertainty day after day. Elaborate conventions for the treatment of pilgrims are common along ancient pilgrimage routes, buttressed by both mundane and sacred forces of this world and the other. Even so, extended, voluntary exposure to danger can reveal much about the pilgrim's habits, judgments, impulses, and unexamined beliefs and expectations—rich material for self-knowledge and transformation.

So, yes, a pilgrimage can initiate or deepen a process of inner transformation, but the pilgrim is unlikely to harvest much fruit while on her journey. A pilgrimage is usually too brief and too full of distractions for the painstaking work of healing the many layers covering the deepest reaches of the person. But it is a great gift to be on her way.

The ancient myth of the underground journey, however, can be a helpful guide for the pilgrim intent on wresting the most meaning from a pilgrimage, for she asks her physical body to do what her inner spirit is also meant to do: move through a complex landscape with as much clarity and integrity as possible and to discard heavy social and emotional baggage as she proceeds. In the process, may she recover the basic freedom and ease of her original Self, her deepest heart.

Approaching the Tender Heart

Manjushri

The student, perhaps reluctantly resigned to the descent into the darkness, steps cautiously down the path. Curiosity has been left up on the surface, along with an unconsidered sense of self-confidence and safety. She enters the unknown, having overcome her resistance and the well-meaning inner argument about the foolishness of deep self-inquiry and self-exploration. After all, there have been very good reasons for not doing this in favor of maintaining a pleasant visage and cooperative manner. Agreeing to the inner journey of transformation has been ridiculed in her world. She has been taught that this is literally "none of her business." With the first hesitant step, she is testing the resilience of those family and community strictures.

She will discover that those strictures include a whole sack of what she will later name "false teachings." She will discover that, one by one, they served as the foundation stones of her personality. They shaped her emotional life, her perceptions, her relationships, her decisions, and her most elemental ways of living her life. That they eventually would reveal themselves as false teachings is utterly devastating. Now that she sees them in the harsh light of day, how can she possibly live her life?

But we get ahead of our story. She takes her first steps into the darkness, down what will emerge as a spiral passageway. It will seem to her that she is literally going in circles, arriving at her starting point again and again. But she is assured, as she circles the spiral, that she must address the core issue from many angles. Nothing less can provide the deep clearing.

Helplessness and discouragement accompany her. As she peers more deeply into the depths of who she really is, she is overwhelmed by sadness, grief, and anger. She then receives her first gift: tears. Even tears had been denied her, as a child. She was rebuked for expressing sadness, and speaking her anger was dangerous. By the time she could read and write, she had learned to silence her feelings. She became "the easy child," the one who required so little of the adults around her.

We describe our seeker's childhood to help the reader understand how a young person might accumulate many layers of self-protection over the years. It is no wonder that peeling back those layers is so challenging and requires such dogged persistence.

But as she walks on, she doesn't know any of this — not the pattern, not its structure or origins, not the challenges, and not the heartache. We see her, though, gather up her courage step by step, motivated by her suffering and deep unhappiness.

Sometimes it is simply too much, and she sits down by the side of the path, unable to move. Her work may suffer. She sleeps poorly. Going to the gym is impossible. She can't understand why a dear friend doesn't help, and her friend wonders what in heaven's name is happening to her reliably cheerful companion? She is overwhelmed by loneliness and cannot understand why there is no kindness or help from her friends. She sits on the path and weeps bitterly for herself.

Weeping for herself is the first moment of healing. She has been led to a moment of self-recognition, and then been given the gift of tears. She grieves for that younger self, and for her exhaustion and despair. Eventually, the long silenced younger self weeps the old tears buried deep within and denied for decades.

She might linger here a long time—weeks, months, years, even lifetimes. Uncovering the buried emotional life and bringing it up into the light of awareness is hard, meticulous work. She must acknowledge her current suffering and accept the invitation to dig down to its roots. Old repressed emotions—especially grief and anger—surface. It can be explosive, a volcano of long ripened feelings, or a swamp of indistinct rumblings. The old containers shatter into a thousand little pieces. Who is this person?

Each false belief leads to more discoveries, and each discovery releases its own deep pain. Some will destroy the reigning story of who she is. It can be utterly devastating. In full view, the conscious self falls apart, shattered and useless. The familiar world fades away. The healing is underway.

No one can approach another's tender heart until she has discovered her own. This is an enormous problem in your culture, with its insistence that self-care is simply not acceptable—certainly not this kind. So much of what is so dysfunctional in your society comes from this shortsighted prohibition. No one can offer to another emotional or spiritual guidance, unless she has already given it to herself. No teacher or guide can lead anyone any further down the path than she herself has already gone. Every culture and religious tradition recognizes this.

So, the student must begin by approaching her own tender heart, which is also to say, her own heart center. It is tender, because it has been stripped of its many layers of defenses. The long Spiral Path has led to many moments of grief and anger, and all that had to be released. There have been many seasons of weeping.

Often, those ancient emotions have been stored in the body, causing illness and other physical problems. Those too must be tracked down and released—a long and arduous process by itself, as the body organizes itself around these deep hurts. Full release often requires skilled assistance. When this is done well, both body and mind are more at ease, grounded and in balance.

These are the tasks of the underground journey, and each task teaches a lesson. One stubborn theme is that you cannot rely on little self for help. Help always comes from an unexpected quarter. Ego is of little use, you learn, over and over. But this eventually will reveal new insights and sensitivities emerging into view.

Gradually, after many rounds, the traveler learns she can relax and trust that support will arrive, from within or without. She has reliable access to sources of insight and wisdom that she had never even known of. She is astonished and curious. More false beliefs wither and vanish.

Each person's path is different. Each person encounters different obstacles, challenges and tasks, which reflect her own personal history in this and previous lives. It may be a brief journey—days and weeks—or a long one, stretching over many years. She may walk with expert guidance or walk alone. She may suffer grievously as she discovers what lies at her very core, or she may find release and well-being with surprising ease. There is no one pattern, and so, this story can only be told as myth. We re-tell it here with a light hand, in simple language, that it might be of use to many students who are embarking on the greatest adventure of a life.

And so, she persists in the meticulous and painful labor of peeling back the thick scar tissue protecting her tender heart. She is barely aware of the transformations underway. She is startled to recognize the unlived life, barricaded paths, silences, and barely contained rage—suffering upon suffering upon suffering. What to make of all of that? Who am I? How do I even move through a normal day, now knowing this about myself, whatever "myself" even refers to?

In the midst of such confusion and disorientation, she will also catch a glimpse of her tender heart, there at the center of her being, radiant with light, untroubled, whole and entire within herself, undivided and at ease with all. This is the home of Spirit, the source of the energy animating her life. Microcosm and macrocosm, to use a favorite image of your Western cultural tradition, mirror each other; what is within and what is without flow easily across a porous membrane.

The seeker on her journey has no idea what she has seen or now met—this often named but never adequately described shining center of every being. It is named anima, Soul, Spirit, the Sacred Heart, Infinite Wisdom, fundamental Buddha nature, and the Jewel in the Lotus. It has no discernible shape or form, no density that could be measured, and no coordinates of its location. Yet this heart center is more powerful than any organ or creature, more perceptive, more insightful, more capacious, and more sensitive than any other aspect of a life in form.

Why is it called "tender?" Because it is open to the universe, and because it is the gateway for the flow of the great compassion. In the presence of such absolute fullness, (and absolute emptiness) little self falls silent. Human purposes and worries vanish. Time and space seem to have melted away. And perhaps that is true. There really is nothing more to say.

In the presence of her heart center, the core of her being, she knew, she **had** to know, that all she had sought, all that had led her on her journey in the first place, all that she had pursued and valued and hoped for—all that is fully present within her. At the outset, what she sought seemed to be well beyond the self, and for good reason. She must move into her world first, looking. Then, disappointed and full of heartache, she returns, and eventually, if she is blessed, turns inward. And there it is, the shining, tender heart, beaming light and kindness and well-being in all directions.

The heart center within is tender because the very nature of being is tender. Struggle and force are not fundamental energies of the universe; nurturance, growth, and the cycles of life and death are the fundamental energies of the universe. Beings in form are meant to flourish. The tender heart expresses this in its fullness, and you learn this by approaching it. There really is nothing more to say to you this evening. Light a candle and breathe with the world around you, breathe with the deep rhythms of the lake and the tears and laughter of these days.

I had turned off my computer, but there was more.

Why yes, of course, these days and weeks of grief and tears cleared the way for this Teaching. It could be no other way. Tears lubricate the path to soul and nourish her growth. The most powerful way to dissolve emotional scar tissue is to soak it in tears. Grief, conscious grief, named, expressed, and wrapped in compassion, is the royal road to waking up, to healing and wholeness. Tears should be welcomed with flowers and song and candlelight! Thank you for writing down these last words.

Energy and Healing

Manjushri and Penny Gill

I come to you today because I'm hoping for a Teaching on energy. You have given me many Teachings on healing these last years—healing of body and spirit, healing of relationships, and even healing of community and the world. I'm beginning to understand that energy—inadequate, distorted, disordered, and untended—lies underneath every aspect of healing. There is so much I don't know or understand, and it is becoming ever more clear how central energy is in these remarkable Teachings. I think I need a whole curriculum on energy. It was not very many years ago, when I asked a group of friends much more knowledgeable about these matters than I was, what really is this "energy" you keep referring to? They looked at me in silent astonishment. In What In the World *you taught that we are bathed in a great Shower of Spirit, and that this means, among other things, that we are invited to raise our skillfulness with higher frequencies of energy. I understand that as a metaphor, perhaps, or a visual image. But I don't understand it fully enough, or how it shapes my life and my insights and observations.*

Actually, beloved student, that is not really accurate. You have become much more aware of how energy shifts within you, and you have learned, sometimes reluctantly, to accommodate to it. It was as if you were determined to run experiments on your own mind and body, to see if energy from outside your body could impact the energy available to you, in your body. Being among the trees or next to the lake has answered that question for you. You've also studied the reverse of that question: how some people or situations can drain energy out of your mind and body at an astonishing rate.

So, what do you conclude from that? First of all, energy is real, and only energy is real. Even matter is only condensed energy, and will revert to energy at its dissolution. You also know that the planet is bathed in great oceans of energy swirling about from various dimensions of the universe. You wonder if those swirlings are coherent in any way, and if so, might we infer intention there? We have answered that profound question several times. Yes, it is all energy, and yes, it expresses its coherence, and yes, it has purpose or intention, though not in a simple way comparable to that of a human being.

Human beings have become extremely skillful at blocking most frequencies of energy. One strategic purpose is that body and mind survive. Only a narrow range of frequencies can be tolerated, and there is ample evidence of how evolution reflects that. You can access a narrow range of visual and auditory frequencies, for example. This has short term and long term survival advantages. Your cells only tolerate a narrow range of frequencies as well. High levels of radiation, for example, are lethal to cells. All this you know, and you do not find it confusing.

What confuses you is how certain frequencies and their receptors interact on a non-visible or non-material level. And this is exactly the arena you've been invited into lately. Ever since you moved to the island, you have been diligently clearing out blockages to receiving a wider range of frequencies. That has allowed more ease receiving our Teachings, as well as expanding your access to the vibrational energies around you—among the trees and with the lake, for example. You have noticed how frequently you think of someone, and the thought is followed by a call or an email within a few hours. You are picking up that person's intention, before she has acted on it. It barely surprises you anymore. That, by the way, is not an example of synchronicity. It is a direct sending/receiving of an energetic pulse with a recognizable "signature." You might think of it as akin to a quantum event. This is also how prayer on behalf of someone has a subtle yet powerful impact.

What is most fundamental, however, is that this is the matrix, which connects all beings. This is the fundamental reality, which shapes and upholds all sentient life, and much else, in truth. You say some words to your dog, and she responds effortlessly to the vibrations of your emotional energy. You ask the circle of trees around your home to hold you, and their roots send a signal through their underground circle of connection, embracing you. You pour out your lament to the Great Lake, and she effortlessly receives your distressed energy and sends calming vibrations to your heart. These are real events, real processes palpable to anyone who pays attention with an open mind.

Ah, and now you notice that your own energy is flagging rapidly. So we will stop now, and continue at our next session with a Teaching on receptors. Yours have stretched this hour to receive this Teaching, and now they are full. You have been receiving a much higher frequency of energy than you work with normally. Soon we will speak to you of practices, which can help you increase your availability to higher frequencies. Until then, please study this Teaching, which has been mostly a summary of what you learned last year.

It is not an exaggeration to say that a major component of what you call healing is actually a process of gaining more and more sensitive energy receptors, to a wider range of frequencies. Let me explain that to you. A human person is composed of or contains multiple energy systems. Some fuel cognitive and physical activities, for example, and some are engaged in complex regulation of other bodily and psychological processes. Some are scanning the environment for danger and opportunity, and some are processing the continuous flows of information from without and within. All of this "work," for energy does work, requires food and rest in order to function well.

When a person needs healing, it is because there are obstructions to the maintenance and replacement of these many, interconnected energy systems. That is actually what healing is, in its simplest terms. Obstructions must be dissolved or released, which allows energy to flow freely through its channels, thus enabling it to fulfill its function.

So, the intricate and sometimes very long work of removing obstacles to the easy flow of energy within a person and her several energy bodies can be the difference between life and death. It is certainly the difference between just being alive and flourishing. These obstacles, which we have discussed with you many times, can be emotional, karmic, mental, physiological, or environmental. A skillful healer must first assess that initial question, before suggesting a healing path.

The path of healing then is often a path of deep transformation, as described in these pages. This deep healing almost always results in enhanced life, for these newly activated energy receptors allow more ease, patience, and calm. One might say, there is even more sanity!

In a sentence: healing obstructions and clenched emotional and psychological patterns releases energy to flow more smoothly. Energy receptors can then process energy more efficiently, often of a higher frequency. This becomes a very positive feedback loop, which certainly you now understand.

Why a higher frequency or a broader band of frequencies? Basically, because the organism is less stressed, and so, not at risk. An organism at risk shuts down unnecessary energetic work in order to focus on surviving the risk. Once the healing process is well under way, the organism can relax its emergency controls, and allow a more expansive availability to its environment. It becomes both more receptive and more sensitive to a wider range of frequencies. Many consequences may follow: more ease, more complexity, more insight, more risk-taking, more creativity, more communication, more learning, and more.

You are watching this in yourself. After several challenging years clearing out obstacles and old patterns of self shrinkage, your energies are flowing much more fluently. You recognize this every day. You find new physical stamina, more physical flexibility, and richer cognition and creativity. Your writing has taken off in new directions, giving you much pleasure. You may recognize some physical healing of old, chronic illness. And you already are noticing that you are receiving subtle information about friends and strangers both close and at great distance. Your intuition is gaining depth and accuracy. And more.

Most human beings use a small fraction of their potential for receiving energy, really small. Any way people can expand their receptivity would significantly increase the likelihood of humans solving some of your most pressing environmental and social problems. Please study your own experiences of energy, healing, and expanding receptivity to more energy frequencies, so you can assist others. Though this can seem very "woo-woo" to some, it is firmly grounded in material reality. It does indeed open up realms otherwise not accessible, such as we are doing right now. But for the reluctant, there is plenty of gain to be had within the confines of conventional human understandings. You need only begin by looking for the social rules prohibiting it. Where are the taboos? Who gets mocked for what? Whose interest does it serve, that other realms are relegated to the fanciful and the fictional? Reread *What in the World* to refresh your answers to those questions!

It is the late in the day, but I would like to write out several questions, which I hope you will address some time. I understand that the basic process for improving my sensitivity to energy, including higher frequencies, relies in part on removing obstacles lodged in my body, psyche, and emotional life. Fear is undoubtedly at the top of that list. And, I would think, blocked energy systems limits access to energy, which could lead to more obstacles. An illness can lead to depression, and depression can lead to more illness. There must be many versions of such unhappy cycles. I would appreciate further explanation of this and more suggestions for how to interrupt those cycles and begin the healing.

My last question this evening is this: In whose interest is it that most of us fail to receive higher frequencies of energy? Obviously, anyone who wishes to constrain my freedom of thought and action, my confidence in my own insights, or my willingness to take risks. That could include political and social institutions, which would prefer to keep me under control and compliant. But are there more?

Oh, you political thinker! Actually, this is merely a small part of the vast fabric of modernity, with its devotion to materialist views, economic gain, and scientific epistemology. There is no enemy here, and no opponent you must battle. You and many others are the leading edge of a great transformation of human consciousness. It is truly in everyone's interest that you carry it forward as far as you can, and then, return and continue. Despite what you believe you see all around you, it is the arc of human history.

Despair: A Teaching Story

Kwan Yin and Penny Gill

Oh, Kwan Yin. Something tough happened to me tonight. I broke open in a swamp, a tidal wave of grief like I've never experienced before. This wasn't just weeping. I wailed, and I couldn't stop for hours. I'm exhausted and drained. I warmed a little bowl of rice, and then watered the very dry garden.

What triggered it was absurdly insignificant. I was unable to add a new email to my Gmail account. A two-minute task I couldn't figure out, after wrestling with my new web site. I'm worn out with the details of the tech world and its impenetrable language. And I know I must master it because of its vast power to bring the Teachings out into the world.

And then, the deeper misery: there is no need for a new website and book. There is already a surfeit of Teachings flying about the Internet. I've nothing helpful to add, and no one has time to read, anyway. None of this work matters. Human beings are hopelessly lost, and I am utterly insignificant. I'm lost in the terror of this dissolving world just as everyone else is. The markers are gone. This is beyond disorientation. At first we noticed it in our outer, shared world. Now it is within each of us, like a silent virus. We must face it alone.

Why wouldn't I howl in pain? We are so lost, as we hurtle helplessly down this path of self-destruction. We are drenched in fear. We have forgotten what we knew. Few are paying attention. Most of us huddle in our tiny huts of ignorance and denial.

Who can help me hold this terror and grief? That led to another round of distress and a raw sense I face this alone. My calmer mind knows that we are all in this together, and that many struggle for language to name what is happening. I am certainly not alone, not empirically. But emotionally,

I'm devastated by the loneliness, and I am crazed by my need for care.

Is there language for this? Is there some way to name this grief or what is happening in our world? That urge to name, to distill this into language, is so fierce, surely because in some way I believe it will help me wrest some control, some understanding, and even, God willing, some meaning from this devastation and destruction.

So, I ask you, beloved Kwan Yin, for a Teaching. I need to find my footing and return to my more stable self. You have taught me about my heart center and its deepest life in Spirit. You pour from your great vase kindness and healing. We all need this. I long for this healing, and then, to be able to share it in my world.

What is happening to our hearts? How can we protect that tenderness within, which keeps us alive in our deepest humanity? Can we heal ourselves, so we can even imagine being able to offer some salve of healing to those around us?

The best I can do tonight is to haul some of this anguish into language, so I can ask for help. Anguish is a good word. It is also profound disorientation, as if I've been dropped into an unrecognizable reality. All I know now is that bare feet on the ground is good. Breathing is good. Sitting under the swift clouds and the bending birches is good. And then?

Oh, dearly beloved Pennyla: yes, bare feet, birches, and breathing. Perfect medicine. Big sky and calm lake can hold your grief. You are a human being, thankfully. And only a human being, also, thankfully. Your life is to be a light of kindness and wisdom for others. But you have collapsed now, fearing there is no source of kindness or wisdom adequate for this moment, not in your heart nor in the life of your country. All you can see is life struggling to survive and minds striving to understand.

It is a perfect example of humanity's greatest gift and greatest challenge, for you live, like all who are fully alive, stretched between the realms, stretched between utter Spirit and utter matter. Your bare feet are on the earth and your hearts are broken open to the full force of Spirit pouring through.

Who would choose this as a life form? Only the slightly crazy ones—the prophets and the artists, the poets and the mystics—all you who insist on holding the realms together, one in each hand, juggling, tossing, hiding, howling, dropping, holding, dancing, weeping, balancing, rejoicing.

This *is* what it means to wake up. To recognize, in its terrible vitality, the power of the life force, the fragility of being in form, the awesome potency of mind, the terrifying refusal to embrace dualisms, the ground of awareness, and mystery. Your human minds are pretty small, you know, and they are nowhere near up to the task of taking it all in, which is what they desire more than life itself.

The Dalai Lama teaches, every single day, the infinite blessings of being born in a human life. Our lives, simple and easy compared to yours, are free of the friction and anguish of your lives. But a human life can give birth to vast consciousness, which seems to be the longing of the cosmos: to know itself, to recognize the whole fabric of all that is.

We, the inhabitants of our non-earthly realm, the one you taste but do not inhabit, have a more monochrome life, if I can say it that way. We do not struggle; we do not doubt; we never know anguish or fear. Though those have no fundamental reality, they propel humans, extravagant in mind and heart, to startling insights and exploits.

You humans, you walking the great and hidden path, you are the jewel of the cosmos. You are like small prisms reflecting the light we pour into your world. We watch, confused by your struggles and your failures to see what is right in front of you. But of course, we, beings not in body, know neither death nor birth, neither space nor time, and so, neither joy nor sorrow.

You are the beings with the fullest lives, with the richest experiences, and with access to all that can break you open into the utter fullness of life itself. To always be full of wisdom and compassion, as we are, is one thing: to find your own way to the fullness of wisdom and compassion is quite another.

Our Teaching for you tonight? Be as fully human as you possibly can. Allow yourself to be broken open, to become shards on the side of the road in your pain, and even then, to wave to the small child you meet there. You will find yourself repaired and whole. Embrace your community and your world until there is only a single breath separating you, and then exhale. And embrace them all again. Know yourself standing alone in the face of the whole swirling cosmos, and then you will be nuzzled gently by your sweet dog.

These are not opposites, dear Penny. This is the fullness of life: messy, chaotic, unruly, distressing, incomprehensible, gorgeous, heart-breaking, and always, always calling on any who can hear, to open and respond, open and respond, until that is the form of your being.

Do not try to think about this! That, for sure, is useless. Be it. Practice it. Pour out into your world grief, laughter, tenderness, rage. Whatever it is, pour it out. Hold on to nothing. Life is in the pouring out. It is the life of the Sacred, of all that matters. This is the healing.

Now. Please go to bed! You said yourself, you are exhausted. Read this in the morning. All is well, beloved Pennyla, all is well.

Diving Into the Unconscious: Shadow

Manjushri

We will now introduce several tools to help you begin to identify and then dissolve the barriers to accessing the shining cosmic Heart Center. Small self has laid down defenses, delusions, and useless strategies in hopes of mastering fear and protecting the self. Working with Shadow elements, projections and dreams, along with practices which assist inner focus, mental and emotional stability, and non-judgmental attitudes are powerful approaches to the unconscious.

First up is Shadow, the largely invisible and unconscious repository in the psyche for aspects of a person considered unacceptable. That sounds simple, but it is not. Shadow work reflects the life-long processes of maturation. Shadow and fear are closely related as well, and we will want to hold both in mind, as we proceed through these next sections. This may look like a swamp of smelly muck, but here lies the treasure of the human heart, opening the way to less suffering, more well-being, and freedom.

Earlier we spoke of the anatomy of the heart center, to help you recognize its complexity and significance. The architecture of the heart center is also a prominent metaphor for many Christian mystics. Labyrinth and spiral and related images point to multidimensional experiences, recognitions, uncertainties, barriers, illusions, and confusions.

The word "Shadow" suggests the sense of being lost in the dark and confused by shape-shifting, ephemeral forms. It reminds us that we are speaking of perception and how one presumes to know she sees accurately. We will probe the chaos of projections, faulty interpretations, false beliefs and ego's creative fictions.

In the midst of a chattering human mind, seeing self and other clearly is such a struggle. So, we must begin in the murky chaos of unreliable perception. Hold this in mind, please. "Oh Traveler on this path: Much of what you think you know is false. You do not know who you are, what you are, or where you are. It is no more accurate than a wild dream image. And that is because it IS a dream image."

"The portal to Spirit within is ringed with fear and loneliness." That came to me this morning, and I finally began to settle.

Yes. Well said. Both emotions—fear and loneliness—arise out of ego's false story. It weaves a narrative world to protect the safety and survival of its human host. There is no such thing as personal survival; humans die and disintegrate. All forms are impermanent. But ego is hell-bent, and I mean that literally, on securing its own permanence. It is impossible, a fool's errand, and a commitment to neurotic fantasy. Leaning into the painful pair—loneliness and fear—releases the adult self from its neurotic enchantment, opening the way to spiritual maturity.

This is core Shadow work. The human Shadow holds the rejected aspects of the person, both negative and positive, harmful and creative. Its contents reflect childhood family values, what is taboo and what is allowed. It is a storehouse of lost qualities and potentialities. Shadow work requires skillful discernment, while holding collective judgments of good and bad off to the side. It can be very challenging, for it may require rejecting the dominant values of family and society. This is also why it can take many years to explore the contents of Shadow.

Supportive or harmful, life-enhancing or life-destroying, Shadow energies must be brought up to the light, made conscious, and then either forgiven and healed or taken up and integrated.

The rewards are significant. First, energy, which had kept this material hidden, is released and available. Physical health and well-being may improve; relationships may be strengthened or allowed to wither, if that is appropriate. Self-understanding deepens and newly claimed freedom may allow new work, new projects, and new ways to be in the world. Ego loses some of its prickly defensiveness, and the new humility brings more kindness and compassion. Daily life is easier, with more freedom and less struggle.

Our lives and yours differ in many ways, as you know. We have more freedom, ease, and much wider consciousness. And we are unburdened by Shadow. We are fully who and what we are meant to be. Meticulous Shadow work can bring you and others into the same freedom and ease.

We turn now to anger and grief, two excellent examples of how to release Shadow energies. A young person may be schooled, by her family's upbringing, that she is never to express anger or grief. Great clouds of each may be buried in her Shadow and her personal unconscious. To allow it to surface takes courage and curiosity. With skill and practice, it can reveal much that has been silenced and repressed.

Anger signals danger and alerts the person to pay attention and quickly respond. With its strong, clear energy, it can deliver information about the moment, but it might also shed valuable light on ancient hurt and rage.

For example, the other night you were irritated that everyone expected you to provide soup for your community gathering, week after week. They rarely took their turn. You knew you were angry, but you also believed it was prudent not to speak of it. It sat there, rumbling in your gut.

Later in the evening, when the group was discussing a story in the book of Exodus, your mental self dove into the Israelite victory song over the bloody defeat of the Egyptians. You connected that with contemporary prejudices against Moslems, and without a thought, exploded vehemently. Rage toward an ancient revered text was triggered by your anger about making soup for too many communal gatherings. Your friends had no idea what was happening. Five minutes later your system had returned to equilibrium; you had drained out the accumulated anger about evenings past and present. Afterward you felt limp, but you could not remember what you had said in the heat of the moment.

I remind you of this, to show you how anger can suddenly erupt, triggered by something quite unrelated. No harm was done that evening, even if it was a bit shocking to some sitting at the table. But it is easy to imagine situations where angry energies gathered up from multiple incidents could be released in a great explosion. Its disproportionate intensity signals its origin in the storehouse of Shadow.

This is one reason anger and other powerful emotions are so difficult to understand. Their roots may be deeply hidden, tangled with other issues, or misnamed entirely. It is difficult to express or witness anger because it seems so reactive and threatening. And it is such a surprise. Calming down afterwards can be extremely difficult until its deep roots in the unconscious, in the Shadow, are identified.

So, any powerful emotion can be an entrance into Shadow. If you notice an unusually strong emotional response to an event, a person, or a simple comment, it may be ripe for more investigation. Strong or disproportionate reactions are helpful clues. Someone cuts in front of you on the road. A clerk is discourteous. A friend ignores your wish to tell her a story of what happened that day. Simple, everyday occurrences. Strong, vivid energy rises up out of your chest, and often, straight into language, and it is hurled out with great vigor. You say something you didn't know you thought, or you use language you avoid, or your vehemence startles or embarrasses you.

What is going on here? You stop and take a breath or two to calm your racing mind and pounding heart. Your body is tense and poised for action. You are preparing for aggression. Another breath. Eventually, depending on its intensity, your mind and body return to an uneasy equilibrium. You ask yourself, whatever was all that about?

That is the perfect question, and curiosity is the perfect attitude. The search is on! There are a few questions to try. Because Shadow material is by definition hidden from the ego and largely unconscious, it must be sought out. And because what gets deposited in the Shadow is material unacceptable either to the ego or to those around her—parents, teachers, or other social and cultural authorities—the Shadow material is labeled "unacceptable" or "to be rejected" or "inappropriate for someone like me" or just "really bad."

Let's return to the person in her post-anger curiosity, asking what her explosion was all about. She poses some questions to herself. What did this situation remind me of? Whose voice was being echoed here? Have I been in a similar situation in the past, where I was unable to speak or resist or argue back? Such questions might elicit a clue, an image, a voice, or a sensation in the body. It might even make immediate sense, with a bright "Aha!"

If it does make sense, approach it with respect and gratitude. Pick it up, as you would a red thread that will lead you out of this confusion. With each pause, stop, pay attention, and ask what might be connected. Is there hurt? Rejection? Emotional bruising? Failure? Betrayal? Hold still as best you can, and then, breathe kindness to your younger self who suffered when that injury was initially consigned to the realm of ignorance and invisibility, the Shadow.

There will be many such pauses along the paths exploring Shadow. Thank heavens, you might say. The gifts of Shadow work are life-giving, for you are essentially recreating your conscious self (another phrase for expanding consciousness) and gracing that enlarged self with new freedom. This is why you must proceed slowly and carefully. Especially at the beginning, the small self must stretch a great deal to take up a piece of Shadow material and integrate it into her self-understanding. But piece after piece, excavation after excavation, and integration after integration, the conscious self becomes ever more capacious and the Shadow realm less and less operative.

At deeper levels of this inner work, you will discover these pathways in the Shadow are actually a web of interconnected views of reality, usually markedly distorted views. The seeker realizes she is unlearning so much, she hardly knows who she is or how to navigate in what was once a very familiar world.

What else is happening? Small self becomes less judgmental of herself and others. She discovers she is better able to be fully present in the moment at hand, rather than absorbed in some fictional story about what is going on—one of the favorite activities of a Shadow-drenched ego.

And most importantly for our work here, it is Shadow material that has hardened into the layers of self-protection which block access to the heart center and its life-changing gifts. Please tell something of your own experience working with projections and Shadow.

Retrieving Projections of Shadow

Penny Gill

Working with projections is another powerful way to identify Shadow contents. When a piece of unconscious material is "ready" to be made conscious, the psyche often projects it out into the world, and, oh so often, pins it upon another person. There it appears, in full view. All people do this, all the time. The challenge is to recognize the projection as your own.

What we criticize in others is most likely something we are or do or think. If we judge others, it is likely there is a powerful inner critic as well. Our meanness or laziness or selfishness can rest comfortably on friend or family, because we prefer it to be theirs, rather than ours. It is extraordinary how rarely we are aware of this ceaseless shifting of responsibility onto the shoulders of others. He or she may be hanging out a convenient hook, but the projection is ours and must be retrieved. It is not so hard to do, but it is miserable, no question. Really? All that awful stuff is mine?

I've retrieved projections I'd happily laid on others and then shuddered when I could really see my obtuseness. A stubborn resistance rises up: Is this really mine, an aspect of me? Do I really have to deal with this, and somehow recognize its origin? Am I really this kind of person? Self-centered? Rude? Clueless? Bossy? And on and on—so many possible candidates. The work of reclamation and re-integration is also endless, it seems. The gifts of this work are powerful, for it is humbling, and it grounds me in reality. It brings more self-complexity and eases relationships with others. It's all good.

We also project deeply positive aspects as well. Falling madly in love is the best example, which closely resembles a youngster's intense crush on a teacher, a successful athlete, or a powerful kid in the neighborhood. These projections can reveal precious images of who we wish to be, or even, who we are meant to be, especially if those images point to distant longings or ambitions. If handled gently, they can reveal valuable information for who a person could become or what she could accomplish.

I've found that the surest sign I'm wrestling with a projection is when my responses to someone are disproportionate—more negative, more positive, or more intense and exaggerated than really makes sense. It requires meticulous discernment to sort through these emotional and psychological mazes. Discernment is really challenging work for me. Talking with a wise friend can be a big help.

The projections that have taught me the most (and challenged me most deeply) still have my attention. I realized how, decade after decade I had identified a new romantic interest in my life as a deeply spiritual person. The projection was apparently psychologically necessary, as I couldn't begin to imagine that I too could be a spiritual person. Of course, no one could fulfill that potent image of mine, and so, reality would eventually emerge, bringing great sadness and disappointment along with it. I finally realized the life-long pattern. My psyche insisted I deal with it, despite my stubborn resistance. I had to retrieve that projection, return it to myself, and start the long work of integrating it into my conscious life.

The rewards of such strenuous work are significant: first, a new chunk of energy becomes available, for it was once engaged with keeping the material well repressed in the depths of the Shadow. Release that bit of Shadow into the light of awareness, and you receive the energy as well. A fine bonus.

There is also more ease in your life in the world. Fewer projections means more realistic encounters and much more satisfying relationships. There is less aggravation and turmoil, less stress and drama, more stability and clear-headedness, more kindness and less attachment. I've noticed better health and more reliable energy. And, visible to every reader here, this very book and the wonderful presence of the Teachers has emerged from my long struggle to claim my own spiritual life and then to create ways to share it.

The last practice for exploring Shadow and the unconscious is dream work. "The royal road to the unconscious" is the most powerful of all, and attending to my dreams initiated me into my most adult self.

Message From the Deep

Penny Gill

I go to the water's edge, and there I see a man walking towards me, up to his chest in the icy lake. He wears a business suit and hat, plus a life jacket. I'm concerned he must be very cold, though he doesn't seem to be wet. His voice is low and somber, and barely audible. He apologizes for bringing me bad news, that.... I cannot understand his words, but I understand someone has been badly hurt. I'm grateful for the information, and I thank him.

This was this morning's dream. I'm grateful for it, as I've been hoping for a message from the deep unconscious about this intense work on the new book. Am I on the right track? Is it the right mix of voices and stories? Will it be helpful to anyone? Am I telling the truth, as best I can?

Whereas work with the contents of Shadow, projected or not, helps us to recognize what lies in the upper layers of our unconscious, dreams can also offer a window on deeper issues and powerful archetypal energies. Dreams have been a major guide for me, ever since I was first introduced to their remarkable significance in my early 30's. A novice therapist led me to Jung's ways of working with dreams, but my real teacher was my London guide, several years later. I began to record my dreams each morning, a practice I have continued ever since. This, in turn, has led to my life-saving practice of journal writing. There are literally hundreds of dream journals packed up in big plastic boxes, as if some day I will want to consult them.

This morning's dream invites several questions: who is this man in the icy, dark lake, and what is his message? Why has he come today, and what is his invitation?

First I must decide what kind of dream this seems to be. There are housekeeping dreams, which comment on simple, every day issues with work or relationships. Those are usually like a tap on the shoulder, to remind me, I'm way off base, and need to make a course correction. Or an apology.

There are instructional dreams, which give me an insight into some pattern in my life or some persistent misperception or misunderstanding. They contribute to my well-being, my healing, or simply my unfinished process of maturation. And there are the rare dreams—how should I name them?—that point to the meaning of this life and the path to fully realize that meaning.

There are the decisions about which interpretive lens to use, when addressing a dream. The temptation is always to take a dream literally. An image of a friend surely must be telling me something about that friend! Hmm, probably not. That image is more likely to refer to some characteristic of that friend which is also mine, or should or could be. Probing your associations with that friend often generates a clue.

In other words, the dream's power lies in its ability to make visible unknown parts of who you are. That interpretive lens considers everything in the dream to refer to some aspect of yourself. So, not only the man in the business suit, but also the life jacket and the lake. You can see how rich and instructive such dream work can be. Fruitful dream work requires curiosity, patience, and time, lots of time. My own dreams have developed their own vocabulary of images over the years, which I've found extremely helpful.

Let me close here with an old dream, which I received decades ago. It returns in some form every several years, as if to sharpen its instruction for me. Each time, I find a new point of entrance or a new insight. The Great Fish dream has been a crucial teacher and guide. I've wrestled with the fish, the knife, the pair of parents, the parental refusal, and the meadow, over the years. Meaning after meaning after meaning has emerged, lighting my way through some very dark times. Years ago I was told I must become the Fish. Just recently I suddenly realized, yes, now I am living in the meadow.

The Great Fish

I'm in a very large kitchen, and laid out on a long stainless steel work counter, perhaps 20 feet long, is a huge fish. I take a two-foot carving knife in hand and slice off a piece of the still-living fish, and offer it to my parents, who are sitting behind me. They refuse the offering. Mother says, archly, "Oh, no, we do not eat fish."

I'm heartbroken for having so unnecessarily harmed the fish. I go out the kitchen door and find myself in an enormous meadow, covered in sunflowers and drenched in light. It is stunningly beautiful.

Healing Fear

Penny Gill with Sir and Kwan Yin

Shadow, projections, and dreams are intimately intertwined with fear. They are often triggered by fear and intended to disarm fear. Fear underlies our many sufferings, and to heal and become our fullest selves, we must eventually address our deepest fears.

I offer here an inside view of an example of profound healing of fears that lay under a great deal of how I understood myself and my life in my world. You will see here a lively bit of ego, dream work, active imagination, adventurous engagement with unconscious energies, and profound teaching and realization. And you will see how struggling with my many fears was the essential preparation to write this book. I had no idea that was the case. Eventually, I learned how conversation and relationship are powerful medicine, especially when accompanied by curiosity and an open mind and heart. You will see remarkable shifts in both voices, mine and Sir's.

An Inner Process

I

Penny: It all began with a tough, strange dream, in which I am being abused by an inner voice, which criticizes me and my efforts to write, and laughs at my hopefulness and excitement. It attacks when I get a clear idea, the creative juices start to flow, and I get so happy. I listen to that mocking voice, and I crumple in self-doubt, defeated.

How many times have I gone through that painful cycle? It's heartbreaking. Can I bring that voice up and engage it? Can I find out what is going on? Who is he? I know it's male. From Yale? That's when it started. I had to learn the new language of the discipline of political science, and it so undermined my true language.

Do I want to do that excavation now? It's like sexual abuse; he rapes my creative energy. The dream offers an image of my soul, and I respond so fiercely. "I'm a woman! Look at my breasts!" The male rapist's response to that nurturing, erotic, female power is to denigrate and mock and then attack and assault. Such an image. So raw and primal. My shoulders are tense, and a great howl of rage is gathering. Whew.

So, who are you? What do you want? Why do you do this to me? It's so destructive!

Sir: I'm protecting you, you foolish woman. You think the world is safe for you, and that you can speak and write as you wish, and that people will respond. You believe you are free to speak from your deepest heart and mind. Don't you realize how stupid and dangerous that is? What is the matter with you, you who are supposed to be so smart? Stupid, stupid—and naive. And you even believe all that fairy, mystical stuff. When will you grow up and see reality as it is?

Penny: Wow, you are really scared and angry with me. We can talk later about what an awful impact you've had on my life, but now I need to know, what are you so afraid of? What danger don't I recognize??

Sir: Stupid naive woman—psssspt! I've been telling you this all your life, and still you argue with me. Now that you're no longer safely embedded in the academic world, you're causing me so much grief and trouble. You endanger yourself when you write this rubbish, especially as if you believe it. No one will torture or hang you for heresy or witchcraft now, but I was around when they did—and even then, you wouldn't listen to me. Women aren't supposed to think or talk with spirits or heal the sick. That is reserved for men. So now, in this life, you violate two natural laws: you claim to be more powerful than I am, and you insist humans share the universe with beings not in body. It is too much, too ridiculous, and way too dangerous.

Penny: OK. I get the ancient fear born of your experience in past lives. But doesn't that suggest I'm right about the realm of Spirit and Teachers and karma and all the rest? Aren't you ignoring your own reality and experience?

A long silence from him, head down, as he takes in my point.

Just because my culture is so obsessively materialistic doesn't mean that view is true. It just means it is the dominant belief supported by the dominant institutions. But look at what a mess we're in! Everything runs on fear! What good is that? There has to be another way to be, or to hell with human life! Literally. For we are creating a hell.

I may not have it right, but I don't want to die wishing I had said something about our world and who we really are. Sure, I'm afraid. But if you could settle down, it would be much easier for me. I'd be able to write what is stacked up inside me.

How can I help you with this terrible, ancient fear? How can I persuade you, that you don't need to get all worked up, just to protect me and us? I'm OK. We're OK. We have everything we need to do this—plenty of time, space, money, and even enough readers to help me along.

It would be wonderful if you'd be willing to help, but that's not necessary. I just really need you to relax and let go of your self-assigned job of "protecting me" by obstructing and even assaulting me.

You raise another issue, about keeping women in their place and denying their powers. This is an ancient and gigantic issue. Let's save that for another conversation. For now, please consider whether you could sit down and relax a bit. Could you just be curious about how this might develop? If you could, is there anything you might be willing to do to help the writing? There is no rush. These are huge questions, and I want you to have all the time you need to consider them.

He is visibly more relaxed. He's young, maybe 20? Hot-headed and impulsive. Perhaps he is grateful now to stop and step out of his panic.

You and I aren't going to fix the gender system ourselves, but we don't have to reproduce it! We can be creative partners. You can't imagine how desperately I need that. That would contribute more to my sanity and health than anything.

Sir: Really? His face is full of amazement. Really?

Penny: You can't imagine what a difference that would make.

Sir: You'd like me to be your partner in this huge project?

Penny: More than like. I need you. Otherwise, I probably won't be able to do it, and I need to do it. The Teachers are calling me to write these books. It is so daunting, and I can't even begin unless we're all moving in the same direction.

Sir: Well...that's a whole new picture. I need to think about this.

Penny: Good. Thank you so much for showing up, and for being so forthcoming and articulate. It was very brave and honorable of you.

Sir: Do you really think so?

Penny: Yes, I really do. So, thank you very much. Let's talk soon.

Sir: OK. And thank you for inviting me out into the light. This was really nice!

Penny: Good.

II

Penny: Good morning to you. What shall I call you? This is awkward, not having a name for you.

Sir: Good morning. Yes. I'll tell you later. You can't know yet.

Penny: OK. I'm so grateful for our conversation yesterday, and for how forthcoming you were. I'm here to listen this morning. Are there other things about me that worry or frighten you?

Sir: Well, yes. (He seems surprised at my question, and not quite prepared for it.) There are many things. You are headstrong and so verbal, and you blurt out things that are very sharp and powerful. They are difficult for people to take in, and it makes them cautious and self-protective.

Penny: Yes, I'm sure that is true. I recognize that. I get so impatient, when someone goes on and on, still missing the point. It's partly because I want to engage more deeply. So, what else?

Sir: That is just a small issue, I know. But the biggest threat now is that powerful voices are inviting you to take up a new life and to allow yourself to be known as a spiritual teacher. This would be even worse than publishing a book. You will be so visible! You will be rejected by normal people and powers. Your college and professional life will be over. Your academic friends will dismiss you and distance themselves from you. What kind of life would that be?

I must remind you how naive and inexperienced you are. You don't know anything about this kind of life or what it would mean for you. It is an absurd risk for an old woman! I intend to make sure you have so many doubts and fears that you will never surrender to its allure. That's my job, and I will do it! (He almost snorts with his determination and self- confidence.)

Penny: Ah, young friend, so you can hear a call to me? It's that substantial?

He blinks, stunned. His confidence drains out of him.

Sir: Well, yes. And it comes from a very powerful, authoritative source, your Teacher. That's why this is such a crucial moment! (His energy returns quickly. He regains his certainty.) We have to turn away from that, and not respond; or maybe we could say: "Not in this life, thank you. Maybe some future life."

I press on, so curious.

Penny: So, do you know what the call is?

Sir: Sure. It's for you to surrender to their energy and give yourself entirely to teaching and healing in the communities where you find yourself. That's how it all fits together—you, your history, your writing, and your teaching. And how you are opening to other kinds of energy—if you say yes to this, I will fight with my last breath to frighten and stop you. If you say yes, I'm done. You are on your own. Figure it out, stupid, naive, headstrong woman!

Penny: I need to clarify something here. If I say yes, does that mean you've been defeated; that you would disappear? Do bits of psyche like you die? Or just ebb away? Are you in truth responding to your own fear of vanishing? Is your fear of consequences for me just the packaging to protect your own viability? Is that why you must desperately claim to be useful?

His jaw drops open, but he has no words. I allow the silence to hold both of us. Then, very quietly, I say: There are many things I need you for. There is no need to arouse this fear and misery to continue to be useful. Let's figure out how you could really help me. Let's each think about that, and talk again soon. Maybe even this afternoon. Try to imagine the best use of your access to other beings not in body, your clarity, and your fierce, protective energy. I know I need support and protection, for these are difficult territories to enter. I know I won't be able to take a next step without support, from inside and outside. So let's each ponder this possibility, and then come together to talk again. I can't tell you how grateful I am for your arrival and your articulateness. I'm so hopeful now. And you've already helped me see how I need an inner partner and support system. Deep gratitude to you. Does this pause to reflect seem OK to you?

He nods.

Sir: Yes. That's fine. There is a lot here I too must think about. You show your healing/teaching face to me, and everything shifts. I must think about that. No wonder they are calling you.

Penny: Good. And thank you very much for that comment too. Tell me when you'd like to talk again.

III

Penny: Hello, Angry Protector. I still wish I had a better name for you. But I'm wondering, are you interested in having another conversation? It's not urgent for me, but it doesn't seem to me we are quite finished. It just occurred to me I should reread our last two conversations first, so I'm clear about where we are. I think I'll type them up now. This is an extremely valuable and significant exchange for me, and I want to take it in.

Sir: OK. That seems like a useful thing to do so I'll wait. I don't like being called Angry Protector, so you can call me Sir.

Penny: I will, of course, but it seems odd. I'm 70, and you are very young, 20 or 25?

Sir: That is how I appear to you, but it isn't accurate, nor is it the whole truth. I can appear in different guises. Sir is appropriate.

Penny: OK. Thank you very much. That makes it easier for me. Before I go type, here is something I've been thinking about. I've been imagining what it would be like, if I were supported for this enormous transition towards a new way to live in the world. If I had helpers, colleagues, or parts of my psyche that would encourage me when I'm frightened, when I want to hold back. I wonder if you'd be willing to do that—to be a protector, but not by opposing and obstructing me. It would be so wonderful if your great strength and clarity were available to me, especially when I'm trying to emerge from my hiddenness or wish to bring Spirit into the room, without cowering or silencing myself. I think then I'd learn how to do that more skillfully. That's the next big thing I need to learn: how to exit from my hiding place. The Teachers, both in and out of body, are asking me to do this.

Sir: Yes, I see that. That's one reason I got so alarmed. You weren't thinking very clearly. You go type. I'll consider this. We can talk later or tomorrow.

Penny: OK. Thank you very much, Sir. I deeply appreciate this.

IV

Penny: Oh, beloved Kwan Yin, what is happening to me? I desperately need advice and help this morning. What is happening in my gut? How should I tend it? What advice is the dream giving me? What my gut seems to want is a great diarrhea attack, to clear out my system.

Kwan Yin: She laughs. Well, that would relieve the pressure. But first, it would be more skillful to be clear about what energy has lodged in your body there, and then to learn how to release it. This is not so hard, and it is a crucial skill for someone on the healing path.

You've called up into a dim light a very active, powerful inner voice, and though you've engaged him very well verbally, he is also in the habit, when desperate, of planting himself in an energy center and causing it to nearly stop functioning. That is what you are experiencing now. He has planted his stubborn, fearful energy in your second chakra, where childhood identities and loyalties are rooted and nourished. That's your basic sense of where you belong in the world. He is disturbing that, mightily.

Feeling unrooted in place has been difficult for you, as it is so often for creative people, such as artists, musicians, and intellectuals. Now, and ever since you first came to the island many years ago, you increasingly recognize your rootedness here. That creates a deep inner conflict, which you are noticing in your body.

Please invite Sir back for another conversation. Ask him about this, as well as your question from last night, about how a part of your mind is creating fear, in order to stop you from your next awakening. This can be a frank and courteous dialogue, as it has been so far, or a ferocious struggle—Jacob and the angel, Jesus in the desert, Buddha refusing to move from the Bodhi tree. This is "eating the dragon" of your fears. This is tough, beloved student. You will prevail because you have practiced this many times. But you will be limp after each struggle, and you will need to rest. And you must stay away from negative energies until you recover, for at least for three or four days.

Penny: Will you support and instruct me?

Kwan Yin: Yes, yes, of course. Your openness to us is what has brought you to this point. It would be impossible for someone who only relied on ego. That's why these Teachings are always in code, lest they lead someone to harm. You are not in any danger, and you will emerge with much more clarity about your self, your voice, your powers, and your work.

Penny: OK, beloved Teacher. Already painful realizations are pushing to the surface. The first is how I've never felt protected or that someone "had my back." Here come the tears. No wonder I'm afraid now, as I'm ignoring all my "rules" for staying acceptable and thus safe. And now, great sobs arise, for that unprotected youngster.

Whew. That came up from some deep place. Yes, beloved Teacher, I can see this will be a tough day. But if there is release and clarity in it, I'm grateful. Please stay with me and guide my understanding.

Kwan Yin: Yes, yes. You are already engaging with the work. Blessings, beloved student, blessings. All shall be well, all shall be well.

V

Penny: Good morning, Sir. I hope you will join me now. I really need to talk about this "protector" piece. I don't want you to stop doing that. I need protection, or maybe more accurately, I need a protector. I never really had one. I was endangered in the family, and then I discovered I could be welcome and safe in school. So I never left school.

It was an excellent solution to that deep childhood vulnerability.

Now, after 65 years, I've finally left school. Without my loyal colleagues, I feel exposed and vulnerable. So I need to trust that someone would intervene if I were in danger, which my parents were unable to do. In fact, as a child of seven or eight, I learned to protect first my younger brother and then my sister.

I do need a protector who scans the horizon for dangers, who can sense difficult energies, and who can suggest skillful means to ensure my safety. But not one who operates out of and generates fear. That obstructs my expansiveness and freedom. That keeps the circus bear huddled in the corner of her open cage.

I'm stunned at how deep this sense of vulnerability is. I'm beginning to see how ignoring that to push through anyway really doesn't work well. This time I must meet it and heal it.

Sir: Well, this creates a whole new space for us, doesn't it? Yes, I'm very willing to talk about this further. First, the reason for your gastric distress is this long week of inner and outer clearing has detonated that profound woundedness in your second chakra, as Kwan Yin suggested. That is the deep well of your fear, for you were never adequately enfolded in family or community. You were the outsider, the interloper, the irritant, and the scapegoat, and you've re-lived that many times.

Lately, these patterns are shifting. You are finding community here on the island, for example, and the new life and new work are slowly emerging. But your first response is caution, reflecting your life experiences of being rejected, even after having agreed to "be of use." I've been fueling that fear, to protect you from another experience of rejection. This is what has brought us to this crisis point. Only now are clarity and healing possible. Do you understand all this?

Penny: Yes, I think so. It certainly gathers up many disconnected pieces into a coherent whole. But I don't know how to proceed.

Sir: That's OK. Besides, you are not in charge. We are, your interior tribe of voices. You seem ready to heal this wound, and most of us are willing to help. There are some very young parts who will need more care. Any change frightens them.

You did not belong to your family of origin. It was a temporary launching pad into your world. Lately, you began to find new local and global communities. You need both, for they will offer you new ways to understand your place in the world. And you may well contribute to a radical vision of profound civilizational transformation.

I am willing to help you grow into this new form. But this is what you must do, if I'm to help you. First, you must consider me your partner and collaborator. You must practice asking my advice.

Second, you must carry the burden of your habitual fears much more consciously, until you have integrated them into your conscious self. Ask them questions, listen critically, and release them with respect and gratitude.

Third, you must learn to welcome opportunities to speak from your deepest heart center.

These three practices will intertwine, until they become fully your own.

Penny: Yes, Sir, yes. I'd happily accept these practices. I really do understand each one, I think. I also know I can ask for help and encouragement from you, from the Teachers, and from a few wonderful companions on the way. I feel support inside and outside for this way forward. I bow in deep gratitude. And I think my gut is already easing. Amazing.

Sir: Yes but there is still a terrified, clenched child there, so soothe her with tea and candles today. You can type this up, if you wish, and then, some gardening, a walk, or a kayak ride. Be careful, as you do not have much energy now. And nothing more substantial than a little fried rice or soup. Let everything rest, please.

Penny: OK. Yes. Of course. And a little niggling curiosity wants to ask you, who are you, this astonishingly transformed voice and presence? Manjushri? Some unknown archetypal presence?

Sir: An enigmatic, tiny smile: Since you didn't ask, I won't answer. But, as in the wonderful question, "a cookie or a kiss?" the answer is Yes!

Penny: Hmmm. Along with waves of gratitude, it seems things are now in their proper place. The turmoil is gone. The lake is calm.

Sir: Excellent. We all bless you! Easy now, easy.

Penny: Thank you, thank you.

Understanding Healing

Manjushri

Healing must be understood on several levels: the individual, her community, the environment, and the grand world and universe where you live. Our central Teaching is that healing the hearts of individual people begins the profound healing of both local and global communities. No one can bring reform and healing to her world until she too walks her healing path. This is very challenging for many people of good and wise hearts. They report, "Well, I certainly am glad to work for change here in my community, but I've no time or energy to tend to my own suffering and inner conflict. It seems impossible, even selfish, to pause and give myself kindness and compassion." This is why we teach what we do. It is the essential step.

Healing dissolves the obstacles to a person's full flourishing. It may require attention on the physical level, though that is rarely its root. That is one reason your country's sophisticated medical treatments can rarely restore a person to full health and well-being. The obsessive focus on the body's symptoms ignores mind, emotions, subtle energies, unconscious patterns, and false beliefs. Deep healing requires a much broader approach.

A child is born with a purpose, which she is to discover and pursue. She must learn to give it form and shape, so it can manifest in the world. This will be how she lives into the full meaning of her life, indeed a blessed life. You have known this, and you've grieved for those unable or unwilling to align themselves this way. The obstacles can be many and fierce and cause much suffering.

Many have pondered the close connections between healing and wholeness. It shaped Jung's work. Marx's theory of historical development ends with a vision of unlimited opportunities for wholeness as the apex of social economy and the end of history. The authors of Torah locate wholeness in the deceptively simple injunction to "love God with your whole heart, your whole mind, and your whole self, and your neighbor as yourself." Jesus may have been a carpenter, but he breathed wholeness, and so was able to share his profound experience of healing. Lao Tzu sketches an orderly world within which wholeness rises out of stability and contentment with little need for judgment or force. Indigenous people—which means "earthy people"—know themselves whole because they belong to the great community of all beings.

You are not whole, because you are not fully free. And you are not free, because you are not yet whole. You require healing. This is true of nearly everyone.

We teach that the path of healing is the path of freedom and wholeness. It can be accessed from many directions. You walk several, and each has been fruitful. It is not a process of addition, but of subtraction. "What must be removed from my mind, my psyche, my emotional life, my simple received understanding of things, so my original life purpose, my unadorned face and my naked self might shine in the light? What might be embraced without fear or artifice?" This is the instruction and the curriculum.

We've arrived now back at the founding myth of your civilization, the people of the Book—the grand story of the perfect wholeness of the Garden of Eden and Adam and Eve's very brief residence there. What was that wholeness, and why could they not remain there? The characters in the myth—Adam, Eve, God, a forbidden tree, and an essential serpent—unfold a story about human consciousness. There are rules about what is forbidden. There is the appetite for knowledge and the curiosity, at the very least, about what is good and what is not. How could they be human, made in the image of that Garden owner, without knowing what is good and what is not? And there is the terror of recognizing their nakedness before the Garden rule giver.

Of course they had to be thrown out! The purpose of a human life, of life in form, is to become fully that form. And that apparently included consciousness of self and other, of relatedness, of wisdom, and yes, of wholeness. Wholeness—fullness of being—for humans could not be without awareness. They simply had to dive into the inner territories of good and bad. Life in the Garden would have been fatally boring, and actually, no life at all. How brilliant they were! Create a little mischief! Juice things up! What is really here for us? And, by the way, what are we? How can we find that out? So, your original ancestors launched you all on the path of becoming whole, but a new kind of wholeness, a wholeness that includes awareness and, on the other side of suffering, of having learned of good and not good. Thank heavens that girl liked apples!

They walked out, hopefully, hand in hand, to begin the long journey towards human wholeness. It is absolutely perfect that one of the very last stories in the Bible—which is a collection of very strange stories indeed—is about a Great Tree whose leaves provide the medicine to heal every ailment.

And what of your lack of freedom, now, as an elder and a thoughtful and kind person who wishes to support the healing of others? You do not believe in yourself; you do not trust your own deep voice or its wish to be spoken aloud. It is almost true to say, you hide behind us, your Teachers. You could write every day for the rest of your long life, and not exhaust what rumbles around down there in your depths. You allow it to surface, a teaspoon at a time. The well, meanwhile, overflows. And people are thirsty.

What will you do about this? We await your response.

Years later, the answer to that unsettling question? I am writing this book.

Support for the Work of Healing and Transformation

The path of healing is long and challenging, and those who walk it require support. The personal work is hard; it retrieves painful layers covering the tender heart center and uncovers ancient wounds and fears. There are different methods you might use—many forms of meditation and visualization, for example, such as self inquiry, dream work, body modalities, and more, but each requires sustained attention and practice, great courage, and a willingness to lean into the pain rather than turn away from it. Self-healing is the primary task, and it asks everything of the practitioner.

What else can help? A skilled and personally experienced teacher is nearly a requirement. An insightful teacher knows when to encourage the student to push forward and when to stop and consolidate new information and insights. She will be alert to dangerous moments on the path, such as when the student must grasp a new view to avoid harm. A skillful teacher knows when to offer hope and when to withhold it, when to describe a future outcome and when to allow it to be murky and indistinct. And perhaps most essential, a skillful teacher knows how to keep her student on her path, focused and disciplined and faithful to the work. It is all very subtle, and it requires compassionate understanding and great wisdom.

A community which shares traditions of this path of healing and awakening is a powerful help. Rituals, texts, interpretive traditions, and communal practices can make a critical difference for its members. Well-developed, complex spiritual lineages have created monastic institutions for precisely this purpose. Like the presence of a skillful teacher, a community of practice is a great help and support, a profound benefit and gift, but neither is absolutely essential to the work of heart healing and awakening. There are many examples of people who have walked these paths alone.

What is absolutely essential is this: a commitment on the part of the student to heal her heart on behalf of others. Let me explain. As we have spoken of earlier, the most common reason for commitment to this work, for beginning the great journey of transformation, is to relieve one's own immediate personal suffering. That is fine; it is simply the trigger for recognizing that it is time to take the suffering seriously and to turn toward it in hopes of wringing some relief or meaning out of it.

But the student must learn eventually—and this is often a huge turning point in the process—that she undertakes this work, this underground and often dangerous journey, on behalf of others. She commits to her own healing in order to be able to assist others in their journeys of healing and awakening. She intends to be able to share her newly gained wisdom with others.

But there is a more subtle outcome as well, perhaps not even visible to her. Because all beings are woven together in a great web of interconnection, shifting the energies at one point in the web resonates throughout the system, most potently in her own neighborhood, if you will. But the vibrations move on and on. This, you may recall from our first book, is the phenomenon of the thousand lights turning on, one by one. This is because one person's new awareness can stimulate the awareness of others, for this reflects the fundamental structure of interrelatedness.

To recognize the reality of that structure is to be well along the path. It is a powerful call to serve and care for others. You will recognize this universal ethic in the bodhisattva vow, the many versions of the Golden Rule, and the injunction to be kind to one another as the core teaching of all ethical systems.

There are likely to be many moments on the journey of heart healing when your individual commitment to the work is severely challenged. No healing, no improvement in one's daily life, can be worth this much difficulty and pain, it can seem. Remembering that actually you walk this path in order to serve others is a source of strength, courage, and persistence.

When nothing else seems sufficient to justify the difficult work, understanding that each new bit of clarity or wisdom will be of value to someone else, either overtly or subtly, can often make the critical difference in a student's persistence. Generosity replaces the narrower purpose of self-relief and provides a much firmer ground to the student.

It also marks the gradual shift in ego's authority and power. The seeker may have begun her journey for many reasons, but eventually that motivation must be stripped of its protective coloring. Now it stands ready to support both healing and awakening. This also marks the appearance in the myths and fairy tales of the animal helpers and the natural world, well prepared to help the hero with her tasks and burdens. Many layers of the story now converge, and the student takes a deep turn on the spiral within.

The Radiant Heart

Penny Gill

The Teachers have asked me many times to say more about my spiritual journey these many years, and there is one more topic I must address: my long exploration of more formal religious life. I have imagined it as a thick braid of core elements of Christianity, Judaism, Buddhism, and the Earth-based practices of my indigenous neighbors here in Wisconsin.

Perhaps it isn't a thick braid. Perhaps it is earthy clumps in a great bog, where I have been able to find a foothold for a while, balance precariously, and even rest, until I can take the next step? To tell this story fully would take volumes, but perhaps, after months of procrastination, I can give you a brief map. The Teachers have hoped it might encourage others who walk a similarly complex path. I will try, though it seems particularly challenging: what should be included? What is most relevant? I'm guessing I won't really know the answers until later in my life.

Let me begin with a dream from seven or eight years ago, which seemed to celebrate my long journey. It has remained vivid in my mind ever since.

I am in a beautiful, small, intimate medieval Catholic chapel. A pipe organ graces one wall. Soft light suffused with color from the leaded stained glass windows softens the stone walls. The old oak pews are worn from centuries of worshipers kneeling for their prayers.

On the back wall, where one would expect to find a high altar with a prominent cross, is a richly decorated Tibetan Buddhist shrine riotous with color—reds and yellows and purples. A myriad of butter lamps flicker in the half darkness of the chapel, along with small bowls of fresh water, incense, and vases of flowers, all expressing devotion to the complex images of the central Tibetan deities—the Buddha at the center, flanked by Avalokitehsvara, Tara, Manjushri, and others.

The chapel hums with sacred energy.

I ascend the steps to the oaken pulpit, as I am to give a reflection for a funeral. I stand in wonder and silence.

This Global Moment

We are the first generation in human history to have access to the enormous range of religious and spiritual traditions around the world. We have access to texts, rituals, practices, practitioners, teachers, and communities of believers, thanks to translations, printing presses, wandering scholars, vast global migrations, the dissolution of theocracies and state religions, the inventions of the Internet and social media, and the extraordinary mobility of people around the globe these last decades. Major and minor religious traditions, once confined to one region or another, now are taking root throughout the post-modern world.

It is a central aspect of the many forces of globalization, now manifesting in academic curricula, scholarly pursuits, the culture wars, and the often violent backlash from previously dominant religious institutions. That is not surprising. Beliefs unquestioned for generations must now compete with once-unknown traditions. Young people raised in Jewish households head to the Burmese forests to study with monks. Muslim preachers address the woes of people of color in American cities. Protestant missionaries find rich opportunities among Latin Americans whose countries have been Roman Catholic since the conquest. Mindfulness retreats and teachers rooted in the Buddhist worlds of South Asia show up in corporate training rooms and elementary schools.

Add to that the powerful forces of secularization which undermine ancient religious traditions and institutions everywhere. And the practices and values of science penetrate ever deeper into the global world.

What is a religious teacher, a cleric, a theologian to do?

There are few choices. One can stand one's ground and insist: my tradition has long had it right, so remain here or come join us. You can find spaces for cautious dialogue and non-threatening collaboration. If your tradition is bleeding followers, you could try to offer an adjusted version of your deepest beliefs and commitments.

For the restless seekers, the dissatisfied ones, none of this really works. Not when a great feast is laid out for all to see, to sample, and explore. And perhaps to engage and embrace.

Some religious leaders threaten their wayward members, arguing that they will suffer greatly in this life or the next, if they leave their given religious community. Identity, family, social belonging, marriage and the custody of children can all be at stake. Excommunication—being kicked out of the enfolding community—can be devastating.

I've heard the Dalai Lama say many times to Western audiences that if you can stay in the religious tradition of your family, please do so. It is certainly the strongest root for you. And he pleads: Please do not become a Tibetan Buddhist unless there is absolutely no other viable option for you!

This is wise and compassionate advice, and unusual for many religious leaders, who are more likely to say, "If you are ours, you must stay. Newcomers are always welcome to join us, of course."

I'm sure readers of this essay have heard the scathing critique of those who sample other religious practices or are so bold as to work within two or more. They are mocked as folks who wander along a buffet table, taking a bite here and a bite there. These seekers, they say, must be less mature, less serious, and less capable of meaningful commitment.

I want to reassure these seekers, the restless ones. The unquiet ones. The hungry ones. The heart sore ones. For we are legion, and we are responding to a new era in the spiritual life of our world, with its new problems and its new opportunities.

It is possible that there have always been those who felt this way. But in previous centuries there was little else available in religiously homogeneous societies, and there were powerful forces intent on ensuring widespread religious conformity. Most states had some experience with religious conflict, and many had suffered though long religious wars. States did all they could to prevent recurrences, resulting in few alternatives and suppressed demand.

Until now, this last half century.

My Own Thick Braid

How would a dream of a small chapel, both medieval Catholic and Tibetan Buddhist, be relevant to an elderly American political scientist embedded in a post-modern, neo-capitalist society? It is a shape-shifting story and not easy to nail down. But I will try.

I have been a seeker since I was a child of 8 or 9 years old, growing up in a non-religious, religiously divided family. Religion was an identity or label, but not a world view or a practice. It was always left to me to navigate. I don't recall a single conversation with either parent about any religious subject. My mother was an unidentified Protestant Christian, with a healthy dose of Christian Science. My stepfather had unearthed familial Irish Catholic roots during his long service during World War II. I frankly don't know if either of them was what we called then "a believer," but I do know that one of the few rules in the house was that no one was ever allowed to speak of politics, sex, or religion. Mother eventually converted to Catholicism, probably to protect her marriage; I, child of her first marriage, continued Lutheran Sunday School. Even now, I'm not sure why, except that there was apparently a multi-generational conflict which was resolved by all the parties agreeing I would never be required to become Catholic. So, even as a child, I was free to wander and search.

And search, I did. I have been nourished, in different degrees and over shifting periods, by both Protestant and Catholic Christianity, by Judaism, and by Tibetan Buddhism. Several indigenous practices and understandings that we might call Earth-based spirituality have been consistent threads as well.

In my 40s, I joined the Catholic Church, not because of its theology, but because of its reluctant admission that mystics exist and that mysticism is to be very quietly protected. During those years I received a powerful religious formation, largely rooted in Benedictine monastic practice, with a steady immersion in the history of Christian thought. I said the Daily Office for many years, and went to mass as often as I could, finding deep nourishment there. It was life-giving, and has served to keep me grounded ever since.

Even now in my post-Catholic life, I deeply savor the rituals, particularly the mass. Sacred music moves me profoundly, and I am at home in many parts of both Testaments. The Church and its behaviors? Ah, another story.

I am less connected to Judaism, but I see and hear myself in its stories. I love the fierce voices of the prophets and the psalmists of the Hebrew Bible, and their relentless demand that the community, the people of Israel, behave well towards each other and the land. Almost at a sub-verbal level, those texts have been foundational for me. In many ways, I feel deeply at home in this profoundly complex tradition at the very center of Western culture.

Tibetan Buddhism arrived in my conscious life last of all, though I, like so many, had been drawn to the teachings of Pema Chodron, the Dalai Lama, Thich Nhat Hanh, and others. Its non-theist and non-theological approach to self-inquiry intrigued me, and I began to recognize how my mind and heart rarely worked smoothly together. Buddhism presents powerful and challenging teachings about how to perceive reality underneath all our illusions and false beliefs. I embraced its amazingly clear advice about how to live kindly and generously and sanely in a very complicated world.

I think I saw it as mostly a guide to the mind, even a theory of perception, and hence, of rich interest to me as a thinker and a teacher. And an introvert! Then, as you have read elsewhere, the Teachers arrived—first Kwan Yin and then Manjushri. There is much to say about them and their profound impact on me these last twenty years. A month in Bhutan and Dharamsala and another three weeks in Nepal vividly immersed me in those traditions, and I felt deeply at home in that radically different world.

Several core concepts of Himalayan Buddhism guide my life now: the ontological flimsiness of what we in the West consider to be "real"; the extraordinary power of Buddhist practices to dismantle how we believe our minds and perceptions work; the profound challenge of allowing the bodhisattva vow to shape my life; and the theory of karma and reincarnation to allow for plenty of time to truly wake up. Though I have never really studied its scriptures, gone on a Buddhist retreat, or asked to be a teacher's student, I have found this ancient spiritual path life-shaping and deeply engaging.

Now, in my later years and having retired to a tiny island community with one "church for the whole community," as it names itself, I find myself unexpectedly immersed in a United Church of Christ congregation composed mostly of "refugees" from other Christian denominations. We include many ex-Catholics, a range of Protestants, and even an articulate bunch of non-believers. The back pew is laughingly called "the agnostics' pew." If we consider a Benedictine Abbey to be a version of "high church," then St John's UCC is definitely "low church." It has been a good place to be, for sure, and I'm returning to the Gospel stories to watch how Jesus lived his life. Now, seven decades after Lutheran Sunday School, the way of Jesus resonates deeply for me. Not Paul's theology of atonement, but Jesus living out his life of loving-kindness. I've even been invited to preach there from time to time.

In some ways it seems that I've come full circle, but I've left nothing behind, really, and I have not returned to my starting point. My view has expanded exponentially, decade after decade, until it could hold this indescribable richness of meaning and insight. Follow each tradition back to its founding, and there, among its roots, I have found the common wisdom, the perennial wisdom, which is inexhaustible and life-giving. It is unfathomable mystery. There I find my relatedness with all people and all creation, and, in their company, with the Unnameable, Source of all that is.

I thought I understood this well, and then, not long ago, I received a profound image of what this might actually mean. I close with a brief report. It is probably no coincidence that I received this on Holy Thursday, when Jesus celebrated the Passover with his friends—the central celebration in both traditions, Jewish and Christian.

A Greeting from Jesus

In the depths, beloved sister, in the depths, in the very heart of the Holy, Source of all, We are one. Your beloved Teachers, your Guides and Caregivers, We are all of one heart, flowing with compassion, with All that is and can and shall be.

You too and countless others, all who would know Love, are also here, our energies streaming in and around and within. We are many; We are the forms open to the energies of Love. And there is no separation, none. There is dance, movement, fullness in all ways—all held in perfect silent awareness.

This is True. These beloved energies are the Fact. The myths and stories, the dances and drums and chants, all glimpse this and beg to respond. As do you, our sister, and the innumerable beings who join you, their hearts longing and their minds prostrate.

Such it is, to live in form. Such it is.

Part IV

Last Teachings:
Flourishing in These Hard Times

It is time to bring this book to a close, with a last Teaching from each of the three voices. Manjushri begins with a deeper discussion of energy, and how energies are intensifying and arriving in higher frequencies. Of course, this presents both challenges and opportunities to us Earth dwellers. Next, Kwan Yin has chosen to abstain from language entirely, dropping me instead into a profound experience of that pulsing wholeness of the cosmos, as so many binaries melted away. And last is my brief review of our long journey together on this dazzling, confusing, and ultimately mysterious Spiral Path of healing and awakening.

Shower of Spirit

Manjushri

It is time to ask you again, honored Teacher, to tell us more about our world: what indeed is going on? And how are we to live well and fearlessly in its midst, in these our precious human lifetimes?

An excellent question, for much is in transition, and the attentive students wish to stay in alignment with these energies. In a sentence, this is full blown Shower of Spirit. Our first Teachings for you, years ago, were meant to mentally prepare you and your readers for this profound infusion of new energy and to alert all of you to radical new views of the universe and new opportunities for consciousness. We focused then on some preliminaries, and invited you to pay attention to all that obstructs your awareness and your responsiveness to such phenomena. We grouped those barriers into a long discussion of fear, its origins, its forms of operation, and helpful strategies for eliminating those patterns and habits.

This has gone well, and it has been well received. Now, this second book develops those Teachings in several ways, which we hope will be useful to the students. It focuses on deep healing, for your world and country and community are all in need, terrible need. The suffering is deep and widespread, and the emergence of new forms of communication has led nearly every person alive to recognize this. Never before have so many understood the profound reality of human suffering, in the heart of every person. It is a remarkably auspicious time, and the Teachers are full of joy.

Many people around the world recognize two aspects of this planetary transition: it is manifesting in the realm of human awareness or consciousness, and it offers a vision of the interdependence of all forms of life. Your world is abloom with countless spiritual practices and teachers, who reflect a stunning variety and creativity. There is a path or a practice or a dominant metaphor for every living person — truly a remarkable situation! The challenging aspect of all of this is the speed at which the planet's very atmosphere is changing, forcing adaptation upon every species of life — plant and animal, tiny and huge. There is no escape from this pressure cooker of a world, and many are unable to adapt quickly enough. Your world is transformed from within itself, in full view of all. For some, it spurs attempts to calm the heating of the planet. For others, it feeds the old responses of denial and blame. That divide also marks those whose consciousness is available for transformation, and those who will "sit it out" until a future incarnation. Learning difficult things can be very slow and arduous, and you are watching that everywhere. To avoid your own fall into despair, you must practice a much wider view, especially of time. It will take lifetimes for some people to see what is right in front of them, but their full engagement is not necessary for the rest of you. Send them encouragement, and help them with their deep fears, as best you can. And then, let go.

So, what is this beautifully named Shower of Spirit? We teased you a while ago, saying you had apparently imagined it as a lovely soft soak in a gentle rain. Ah, no. Perhaps "shower" is not such an apt word. Perhaps now we should call it a tsunami, a volcanic eruption, a palpable shift of cosmic tectonic plates, or a flood reminiscent of the story of Noah? The language must capture its tremendous power, its range, its relentlessness, and its cosmic origins.

Yes, we recognize we are sliding into the long human tradition of apocalypse, of end times, of destruction and new beginnings. But that is not what we see. For all those images arose out of a deep awareness of evil, of sin, of human corruption and ignorance and depravity. That is absolutely not the situation, not at all. That is the widespread temptation of despair. No, that is not an option now, not for any whose path is shaped by expanding awareness.

This is not a vision of destruction. It is not loud or aggressive or violent. It is born out of human silence, emerging without force within the heart centers of countless humans. It is the path of healing, of dissolving fear, and of welcoming kindness. We must teach you about Spirit, for this is the unstoppable incursion of Spirit within the existing forms of consciousness. Less than a "shower," it is more a flood rising up from the very roots of life itself. So many of you are already drenched to your knees!

You live in a three-dimensional world, with time imposed upon it. The reality of Spirit is not contained, cannot be contained, within three dimensions or time. This is so difficult for humans to grasp or even imagine. The realm of Spirit has always held or contained the human realm, the realm of planets and physical beings and forces. This is the realm so aptly described by Newton.

Apparently, this little experiment of the cosmos required its own protected space, perhaps something like one of those glass Christmas balls with a little scene inside it. Shake it, and it seems to snow! The experiment has gone so very well, in its protected enclosure.

Imagine, then, that that enclosure becomes porous, and that its environment of Spirit, of that fundamental energy of the cosmos, begins to seep in. Or, imagine a multi-dimensional space intersecting with the Newtonian, three-dimensional space known to you, with an infinite number of points of contact. You could name it, Indra's Net Gone Wild!

How could an earthly mind begin to comprehend such an event or reality or process? That would be as if we asked your puppy to please write a sequel to Bach's B-minor Mass!

Please let this just settle into the back of your mind. You will begin to see countless connections — abstract art, astrophysics, multi-dimensional geometry, literary forms never seen before, avant garde music, and much more.

This is an important Teaching for you and your readers. We will help you to send it out into the world. But first, we will teach you more about Spirit, the other part of that signal phrase. We wish the students to be able to live safely and joyfully within this framework. There is immense freedom here, for all of you.

Heat, of course, is energy, as is Spirit. As is life itself and the visible world where you live. Energy manifests in an infinite range of frequencies, and that simple fact stands at the origin of temperature, form, vibration, sound, and life in all its dazzling variety. Spirit is its primal origin; it is what released what cosmologists name "the Big Bang." Every creation myth around the world starts with the emergence of light, the creation of light. It is a powerful intuition of this beginning, which cannot be known. And it is this "beginning which cannot be known" which we name Spirit. It could also be named Source, but Source as active energy pouring out into the now-emerging space.

All this is unknowable, not only to humans, but also to us, we who live in other realms. We too bow before its magnificence and its mysteriousness. At the most fundamental level, being cannot know its origins. We share with you awe, wonder, and rhapsody. We too resonate with the deep vibrations of the cosmos. It is why we are able to communicate with each other, even across these vast spaces.

How does this help us speak of Spirit? We have said to you before, the cosmos—the energy of Source—intends, always a tricky word as we always remind you, intends for life in form to flourish. Indeed, Source intends life, for it intends all the manifestations of energy, life and not-life. We often name that compassion. And this is why, just to gather up some loose ends here, we have taught you how fear causes blockages and suffering, Then, we've explained how to heal the blockages to the vast compassion of Spirit and its energy, its warmth, its power to enliven, and its gifts of insight and ease and freedom.

We will return to warmth shortly. But first, please remember, that every spiritual tradition offers a path of healing in the service of compassion and wisdom. The paths are many, as you know, but the initial heart longings and the ultimate destinations are one. Truly, all of humanity at all times shares that longing, whether aware of it or not. And because you share this, you are related to every other person, without exception, and they, with you. Recognizing this is the path of awareness, and then creating a world from that realization is the task. This literally says it all.

One mark of Spirit is warmth. Your language is full of this insight: You warmed my heart with your call. I feel warmly towards her. With the warmth of spring, plants emerge. Etc. You already know, warmth signals more life energy, more flourishing, and more abundance.

Except when it doesn't. Except when it signals danger. And so you face the paradox of Spirit pouring its high energy into your earthly world, prompting an explosion of seekers, contemplatives, reformers, visionaries, and lovers of the people, while your planet is rife with wildfires, drought, rising oceans, pandemics, and unimaginably vast suffering on every continent. There seems to be more warmth than the planet can absorb and use, essentially because of human activity. Meanwhile, another form of energy is drenching earthly life, stimulating great expansions of consciousness. Compassion and wisdom are flourishing. Eventually, that will enable people to counter the human contribution to planetary warming. But at this moment, there is a great gap between knowledge and appropriate responses. Plenty of people recognize this. What is to be done?

You already know what must be done, on the concrete level of public, daily life. Reduce the consumption of stored energy such as fossil fuels and rely on the more than adequate sources of solar and wind energy. Reduce in that way the release of CO_2. Limit economic growth, control the outrage of consumerism and greed, and bend your policies towards equity, sustainability, and cooperation. You don't need the Teachers to lay all this out.

But the other dimension must also be addressed—the healing of human hearts to allow for the natural flow of kindness and the recognition of interrelatedness among all beings. That energy flow is what allows the visions of sustainability and cooperation to give shape to your emerging communities. This is not hard to understand. All the resources and skills needed to address their profound imbalance are already fully accessible to you. What we hope is that this vision of their fundamental interconnectedness may release you all from your narrow little systems of blame and rage and fear, of us and them, of all those binaries which prevent you from powerful creative thinking. It must seem like an impossible conceptual leap, and for some it will be. But not for the students. The work now is to open to this great flow of Spirit and expand deep recognition of your interdependence and interrelatedness with all beings. From compassion and wisdom will emerge the necessary vision and determination to resolve the dangerous over-heating of your planet and its atmosphere. It is really simply a question of timing: CO_2 emissions got way ahead of the natural flow of compassion in human hearts. This can and will resolve itself. The students must hold the long view.

Energy is energy is energy. It is neutral. It is itself. It is life, and it is non-life. It is really all there is. This is not about good and evil, not at all. It is not a time for judgment. It is a time for profound healing, for individuals, for communities, for your world. This is well within your reach, truly. Open to this downpour of Spirit and let it energize and guide you. It is the greatest call imaginable, to the fullness of life for all beings.

Showing

Kwan Yin

For several weeks I've wanted a Teaching from Kwan Yin about the Divine Feminine and how we might restore our world's relationship with it and again come into balance.

But nothing has come, not a sentence or even a few words. It was discouraging, one more obstacle to finishing this book.

Now, it is late October, and today must be the most beautiful day of the whole year. A sweeping blue, endless, frames the wild display of color—yellows on the poplar and birch, orange edges of the darkening oaks, crinkly browns of long-collapsed ferns, and maples surrendering their bright red exclamation points.

Over at Basswood Island, a couple miles away, a solitary loon calls out, left behind by his migrating tribe many days ago. There is no response. He waits, and calls again, still hoping for a response. No, no response.

It would be utterly dazzling, even without the Great Lake. But she holds it all in her arms, the stillness unusual in these windy, tumultuous days. The sun is almost too warm on my back, though welcome for the laundry hanging out to dry. I fall out of time.

This is it, I suddenly whisper to myself. This is it. Absolute wholeness, absolute light, absolute being shape-shifting as I watch. And then, even the watching fades away. Like water, I seep into the crevices of my world, into hidden pockets of dark life, and everywhere, all is well. I can barely breathe, catching any movement, any small rustle in the drying grass. The lake laps the stony shore, anchoring the rhythms of inhale and exhale, of every being's breath dancing in synch, signaling to the rest like blinking fireflies.

This is the Feminine, and it is surely a taste of the divine. Source of all that is, sliding in and out of form. Edges blurred. No separation. No doing is necessary or even welcome. That is another realm, not this vast containing that we name the Feminine.

This is her Teaching. A Showing. No words.

My Heart's Desire

Penny Gill

And so, we have come to the end of this piece of the long, spiral journey, the path of healing heart and mind and opening ourselves to the inexhaustible flow of compassion into our lives and our world. We've heard Manjushri's Teachings about fear and how it underlies so much suffering, and we are beginning to recognize the great Shower of Spirit, of new, high frequency energy which is upending our old ways of thinking and doing things. We are gaining glimpses of our profound connections with all living beings, and hoping we will be able to imagine new forms of life, both personal and communal. It is an arduous journey, this Spiral Path, for sure, and long and twisting in seemingly endless loops and repetitions. We begin to understand why we speak of practice, as we wrestle with ancient patterns of denial and illusion. We've been horrified at what we have learned about ourselves, and we have wept bitterly over our grief and heartache. Over and over, we've been reminded to wrap ourselves in kindness and patience, as we struggle to become whole, fearless, and free.

The darkness and hopelessness begin to lift, and we wonder—what now? We know, of course, we will never really leave this profound process of healing, not in this lifetime, and perhaps not in many to come. But what might we now be able to offer to our world? And what do we now understand about our world and how it has built suffering so deeply into its very structures?

We have learned so much about fear, how it underlies most of our most intimate suffering and certainly all of the injustice and violence of our world. Healing our fears, becoming skillful at recognizing how fear continues to shape our lives and our intentions and our longings to be the full persons we glimpse within our hearts fuels us and keeps us on the path. There is hope here, not the cheap hope that expects solutions from "out there" somewhere, but the costly, mature hope that emerges from our open-hearted encounters with suffering and pain. We find confidence in knowing who we are, what we don't yet understand, and in trusting we have those fundamental skills for moving confidently into more and more reality.

As we discard our ancient false beliefs about ourselves and our world, we realize we have also discarded so many burdens along the way. We are literally unburdened, perhaps another way to understand the often fraught word, "enlightened." Relieved of the burdens of unnecessary fear and unnecessary strategies of self-preservation, we see clearly our profound connections with all beings and our mutual interdependence. Such a relief, such a release! We wonder, and perhaps grieve, how long we lived in such confusion. Now, stretching into ever vaster freedom, we find our voices, our visions, and our creative powers.

We must remember, now, to tell our stories to each other, to encourage each other to walk each his or her path, and when it matters, to carry hope and vision for each other.

This is my heart's desire for each of you, and all those whom you love.

Part V

A Parting Gift:
Four Beloved Stories and the Bodhisattva Prayer

I've shared these stories with generations of Mount Holyoke students. Tuck them in your pocket, with my blessing, and as the Irish say, "May the road rise to meet you!"

The Circus Bear

Many years ago, circus trains crisscrossed the United States. The performers and their props were in their wagons, and their animals were in their own cages.

People liked to stroll along the line of parked wagons to view the animals—lions, tigers, bears and even a lonely elephant or two. One evening a small group stopped in front of the bear. She was huddled back in the corner, clearly so unhappy at her life. It was almost as if she knew that she belonged in the countryside there, free to climb a tree and live in the woods. She was, after all, an American black bear, not an exile from the tropics. Something had called out to her. It made her very sad, and the people sensed that.

The next day some townsfolk gathered and began to imagine freeing the bear to her proper world. They gathered friends and kin, and soon they had enough money to buy her from the circus owner. The whole town was very excited. Someone brought a tractor to haul the bear in her wagon out to a perfect place in the neighboring forest. The townsfolk had made a little clearing next to a lovely stream, and there they parked the cage. They left food and water for her, opened the door wide, and left quietly.

The next day, when they went to see what was happening, the bear was still crouched in the corner of her cage, and the food and water were untouched. They spoke kindly to the bear, and then left again. The next day, they found the same thing. The bear was crouched in the corner of her cage, even though the door was wide open. The townsfolk were frustrated and impatient now. Why wouldn't she leave? What was she frightened of? Did she not want to be free?

And so it continued, for many days.

The tellers of the story say that eventually the bear inched her way to the open door, and apparently, one day, just slipped out. But no one really knows, for the townsfolk were so disappointed, they stopped checking each day. No one knows for sure, and as I said, this happened a long time ago.

And so, dear Reader, is there a place in your life, where you crouch in a small corner, too fearful to explore your freedom?

The Great Steaming Pile of Manure

This is a story from my London teacher, which literally changed my life. Imagine her with me now, an elderly Scottish woman in a lovely pastel knit skirt and sweater with gorgeously coiffed white hair. She is sitting in a small chair with a needlepoint cushion. She leans over to me, and shakes her finger:

"Sweetheart," she says (she called all her students "Sweetheart"). "You walk into a room and see there, a great steaming pile of manure, in the middle of the floor. Without a thought you fly into action, to clean it up as quickly and thoroughly as you can.

"This you must learn! You must learn to walk into the room, lean over that pile of manure and smell it carefully. Is it yours? Why, then, yes, please do clean it up. But if it is not yours, just turn around and walk out of the room.

"You may not believe this now," she says, "but when you leave, it will rise up from the floor and return to its owner!"

She was right, of course. It does.

The Rainmaker

Long ago, there was a small village, a village in ancient China, suffering terribly from drought. The plants had withered and died, and the few animals were weak and unwell. The villagers had tried everything they knew, to bring rain to their thirsty land, but none came.

Desperate, the village elders collected the last few coins from the villagers and sent for distant help, a man known for his ability to bring rain. When he arrived, he asked for a small hut for himself, on the outskirts of the village, and to be allowed to rest after his long journey. And so he did. Each day someone brought him something to eat, but he remained in his hut. And there was no rain. The villagers became impatient, because they were afraid.

One morning a small child spotted a tiny cloud, no bigger than his hand, far off in the distant horizon. The next day, it was bigger, visible to all. The third day, the villagers gathered together, hoping, hoping, and yes, the sky was even grey off in the distance. The fourth morning, a few drops fell, and then, there were afternoon showers, and then, a great and deep rain fell, soaking the dry and cracked earth.

The villagers went to the little hut, full of joy and gratitude, and asked him, what had he done, to bring the rain? He smiled gently. "Oh, I didn't do anything. When I arrived, I was very out of balance from my long journey to you. I returned to balance those days in the hut. When I came in balance, the villagers came into balance. When the villagers came into balance, the fields and the animals came into balance. When the fields and the animals came into balance, of course, it rained!"

Tell Your Story Before You Leave!

Many years ago, a traveler came to the border of his great and powerful country, intent on leaving. He carried only a small bag on his shoulder and his walking staff. The border guard stopped him, and then, astonished, recognized him as the revered teacher of the Way.

The border guard cried out to the traveler: "Why are you leaving? Where are you going?"

The traveler shrugged his shoulders. "I'm leaving because I am so weary of these people. They understand nothing, and they refuse to listen."

The border guard, in his distress, pleaded: "Then, if you must leave, please write something, a teaching, for us." And he brought out parchment and brush and ink and handed it to the traveler.

The traveler shrugged again, took up the brush, quickly traced some characters, bowed, and left.

And what did the border guard hold in his hands? The *Tao Te Ching.*

The Bodhisattva Prayer

The Dalai Lama and Buddhists around the world say this prayer every day.

May I be a guard for those who need protection,

A guide for those on the path,

A boat, a raft, a bridge for those who wish to cross the flood.

May I be a lamp in the darkness,

A resting place for the weary,

A healing medicine for all who are sick,

A vase of plenty, a tree of miracles.

And for the boundless multitudes of living beings,

May I bring sustenance and awakening,

Enduring like the earth and sky,

Until all beings are freed from sorrow

And all are awakened.

Acknowledgments

I needed a lot of encouragement to write this book, and I certainly received it! Thanks to my Madeline Island community, which welcomed me into its midst when I arrived here, as a new year-round resident, just a few years ago. Especially heart felt thanks to Marina, Joan, Susan, Gloria, Max, and all the friends of the 4:30 Club.

Friends further afield listened to my stories and eased my labor: Paula and Jim of Leverett, Carol of Northampton, Jeana of West Brookfield, Eva of South Bend, Louise of Marlboro, Olivia of Lexington, Ann of Ashland, Dale, wandering wordsmith, Janne of Norway, and Dr. Jampa Yonten of India.

I rested securely in my writing group of two with Piers of Buckinghamshire, England, marveling at our parallel paths.

Rachel Bauman held my stories, as I wrestled with the profound inner work under way, as I wrote this year. Her wisdom and generosity underlie each page.

And my coach and editor, Jennifer Browdy, visionary and relentless, insightful and respectful, truly a Worldwright, and so kind, brought forth a book I never, ever would have imagined writing, and yet, to my continuing astonishment, here it is.

I bow in gratitude to each and all, for this stunning experience of support and kindness and good cheer. What a year this has been!

Photo by Seri Demorest

Penny Gill was raised in Wisconsin, earned her PhD in political science from Yale University, and taught political science at Mount Holyoke College in Massachusetts for more than forty years. The Mary Lyon Professor of Humanities, she also served as Dean of the College. She now lives in a small island community in Lake Superior, Wisconsin. Her first book, *What in the World Is Going On? Wisdom Teachings for Our Time* (2015), is a collection of Teachings from the Tibetan deity, Manjushri.

Find more of Penny's writings on her website, *Thewisdomteachings.org.*

Made in United States
North Haven, CT
28 May 2022